DANGEROUS PRAYER

Discovering Your Amazing Story Inside the
Eternal Story of God

CHERI FULLER

SHILOH RUN PRESS
An Imprint of Barbour Publishing, Inc.

Print ISBN 978-1-63409-115-2

eBook Editions:
Adobe Digital Edition (.epub) 978-1-63409-605-8
Kindle and MobiPocket Edition (.prc) 978-1-63409-606-5

The author is represented by and this book is published in association with the literary agency of WordServe Literary Group, Ltd., www.wordserveliterary.com.

Published by Shiloh Run Press, an imprint of Barbour Publishing, Inc., P.O. Box 719, Uhrichsville, Ohio 44683, www.shilohrunpress.com

Our mission is to publish and distribute inspirational products offering exceptional value and biblical encouragement to the masses.

Member of the
Evangelical Christian
Publishers Association

Printed in in the United States of America.

Contents

THE POWER OF A DANGEROUS PRAYER

*God is looking for people to use, and if
you can get usable, He will wear you out.
The most dangerous prayer is this: "Use me."*
RICK WARREN

Have you ever prayed a dangerous prayer? It may sound a little scary, but dangerous prayers are actually rooted in the Bible and have been uttered from the mouths of God's people down through the ages. They start when we turn our efforts over to the Lord and are ready to lay down our agenda for His will.

I've observed that when the Lord wants something done, He puts a dangerous prayer in the heart of one of His people. It might be "Use me!" or "Send me!" or "Whatever it takes!" Or it could be a simple but powerful "Yes, Lord!" or any number of prayers you'll read about in this book.

Dangerous prayers are not so much "Bless me" or "Fix my situation" prayers, although nothing is wrong with those. But we're talking about prayers the Spirit prompts you to pray that have the potential to expand God's kingdom, influence others for good, and even bring glory to God.

Like the dangerous prayer Roma Downey, actress and producer, has prayed for many years: "Lord, use me."

Her friend Rick Warren once challenged Roma and her husband that the most dangerous prayer you can pray is "Lord, use me," because He just might answer you! Then you have to be willing and ready to do the work you are called to because you don't know what will happen after you pray those words. She has been praying "Use me" since she starred on the popular television series *Touched by an Angel*.[1]

Eventually those prayers led Roma Downey, in partnership with her husband, reality-show producer

Mark Burnett, to create *The Bible* series that became the most-watched TV movie of 2013. Their twelve-part series, *A.D. The Bible Continues* premiered on NBC on Easter 2015. The series chronicled some of the most crucial, tumultuous decades in history, beginning with the crucifixion and resurrection of Jesus and moving through the events of the book of Acts.

Being able to produce films doesn't necessarily bring a carefree life. In fact, it means Roma and Mark have to be away from home for long stretches of time in faraway locations. It means investing their own money in the films they create without being certain of the outcome. (Downey and Burnett didn't know whether people would be interested in watching a TV series that dramatized the Bible.) Nevertheless, they are committed to letting God use them, and that means working with their talent and influence to create movies that tell the world the good news about Jesus.

I've been fascinated by some of the dangerous prayers prayed by people in the Bible—like Jacob, when he asked God to protect him because he was scared stiff of his estranged brother, Esau, and his four hundred men who were on their way to meet him, perhaps for revenge.

On the banks of the River Jabbok on his way to Canaan, after Jacob's prayer, a man came out of the dark and began to fight with him, a fierce struggle that lasted all night. Finally the angel asked Jacob to let him go before dawn broke, and Jacob prayed a dangerous prayer: "I will not let you go until you bless me." The angel couldn't overpower Jacob, so he touched his hip and dislocated it. As he did, "the hand that touched his sinew touched his soul and changed the supplanter into a saint."[2]

Then the angel said, "Your name shall no longer be called Jacob, but Israel; for you have struggled with God and with men, and have prevailed" (Genesis 32:28 NKJV).

As the book of Isaiah begins, we read a short but powerful, dangerous prayer. When the Lord asked, "Who will go?" Isaiah answered, "Lord, send me." That prayer has been echoed by countless missionaries as God showed them the fields were ripe for harvest but the laborers few and called them to partner with Him to unreached nations and people groups around the world. You see, if we pray and God answers these dangerous prayers, it may stretch us, test us, and take us where we hadn't planned to go. But the outcome may be glorious.

Dangerous prayers require surrender, a giving of all we are to God's purpose. When Abraham, Noah, and Moses said yes to God, lives were saved and nations impacted. Daniel, Shadrach, Meshach, and Abednego's prayers were out of a heart of relinquishment—as in, *We're going to obey You, God, regardless if we perish in the fiery furnace or lions' den or not.* Nehemiah prayed as he pursued what God had put on his heart to do for Jerusalem.

When the angel Gabriel appeared to Mary, telling her that she, a virgin, was going to conceive when the Holy Spirit came upon her and that she would give birth to God's Son, the Savior and Messiah Jesus, she was willing to say yes, even though it was going to be costly.

She responded with a song of praise:

"Oh, how my soul praises the Lord.
How my spirit rejoices in God my Savior!
For he took notice of his lowly servant girl,
and from now on all generations will call me
blessed.
For the Mighty One is holy,
and he has done great things for me."

LUKE 1:46–49 NLT

Many of the psalms are prayers David prayed in the midst of great danger. He could have trusted in great armies and kings, but he didn't. He prayed, "O LORD, I give my life to you. I trust in you, my God! Do not let me be disgraced, or let my enemies rejoice in my defeat. . . . Show me the right path, O LORD; point out the road for me to follow. Lead me by your truth and teach me, for you are the God who saves me. All day long I put my hope in you" (Psalm 25:1–2, 4–5 NLT).

Often we just want to be comfortable and so we give God a list of requests that will make our life, career, or family much better and more successful. But dangerous prayers aren't self-focused prayers. They aren't prayers in which we say, "Lord, bless me. Bless my children. Bless my spouse. Bless my church. Bless my job," although prayers for blessing can be beneficial because we serve a good and gracious God. Dangerous prayers aren't necessarily petitions for our situation to be fixed or our lives made easier. But the good news is they *can* lead to God doing a good or perhaps even a great work through us.

What is the outcome of Roma and Mark's dangerous prayer, "Use me"? They get to work with joy because they know people today are hungry for hope, hungry for something to believe in. Millions of people who have never heard or seriously considered the claims of Christ and the truth of the Bible have been exposed to a life-changing series on screens across the nation and around the world.

Recently I heard the Right Reverend Philip Jones of All Saints Anglican Church in Dallas say, "We're supposed to be somewhat dangerous and pray dangerous prayers, letting the Spirit come alive in us." This kind of praying may usher change or upheaval into our lives as we leave the safety of our familiar easy chair— or whatever our comfort zone is—and embark on what God shows us to do. It may mean reaching out to a grumpy neighbor, serving sandwiches on the streets downtown, writing a song, or taking a mission trip.

What's for sure is that God wants to bring His love, His kingdom, His rescue and power to other people on this earth. And He wants to use *you*.

In the pages ahead I share with you some dangerous prayers I've prayed that have changed my vocation, my focus, and most of all my heart—prayers that took me around the world and that have quite literally changed my life.

You'll not only read about the dangerous prayers of several historical people but also biblical people and individuals who are living today.

You'll read of a teenager whose dangerous prayer was transformative. You'll also get to know a spunky seventy-six-year-old woman who wanted to use her and her husband's life savings to make a home for homeless people in Portland, Maine. All because God told her to, and she said yes.

Which is a dangerous prayer all its own: *Yes, Lord.*

You'll discover the true story of a Muslim woman who, because of praying a dangerous prayer, found Jesus Christ when she didn't even know she was looking for Him. And a story of a man in Oregon who prayed a dangerous prayer for his city and found himself leading a ministry that has done quiet yet amazing things among the poor and homeless.

I've found that some of our dangerous prayers lead to great works and others to small yet significant missions. These simple, short prayers can change our lives and the lives of others. Whether the outcome is large or small is not the point.

When God answers our dangerous prayers, He also intends to work within *us*. As Bill Hybels once said, "You cannot grow as a Christian until you learn to ask for brokenness. Regardless of your level of spiritual maturity, there will always be areas of your life God needs to work in."

The last chapter, "Stepping Out," poses some questions and thoughts to consider as you think about dangerous prayer and ponder saying yes to God. These can lead you to explore the ways His Spirit is nudging you and also help you determine what He's created you for or what may be your next chapter or assignment from Him.

Also included are some insights I've discovered in my years of following Jesus. You might find it helpful to read this book with a friend, coworker, or spouse and then discuss the questions and your responses. You can do that in person at a coffee shop or via e-mail or another social media platform.

Join me as you read the stories ahead in this book. I hope and pray you'll be enriched, inspired, challenged, and perhaps even encouraged to pray your own dangerous prayers.

—Cheri Fuller

Chapter One

HOW PRAYER LED
ME TO PRISON

*Prayer breaks all bars, dissolves all chains,
opens all prisons, and widens all straits
by which God's people have been held.*
E. M. BOUNDS

I looked up at a dark, gunmetal sky as I walked through gray concrete double doors surrounded overhead by layers of razor wire at the entrance to Mabel Bassett Correctional Center, Oklahoma's maximum-security women's prison. The opening of that giant door let me into only the "pen," where I pressed a button and identified my name and purpose. The control officer inside opened the next thick concrete door.

Within a few moments of walking down the path that led to the giant main building, I was in Central Control for the security check. Immediately I was told to take off my jacket, shoes, watch, and belt and load them with my materials bag and notebook onto the conveyor.

Rather than friendly TSA airport agents to guide me through security, two correctional officers in full gear towered over me, equipped with large weapons and big frowns. They barked orders and I followed them. After I'd signed in and my belongings were x-rayed and cleared, I was pointed to the body scanner. I walked through it without setting off the alarm, put my jacket back on, and hoisted the bag over my shoulder, thinking I'd made it through and was ready to go.

I stood alone for a few minutes and finally asked the receptionist to please point me to the C-3 unit building where I was supposed to start a class in fifteen minutes.

"Not so fast," one of the officers said. "Where do you think you're going? You've got to be searched." I hoped it was not his job.

"Wait over there," the other guard added. "You're not supposed to be that close to the door."

Ten minutes later a female officer walked in through another door to pat me down and scan my body to make sure I wasn't carrying any contraband. She wasn't in any bigger hurry than the two male correctional officers were.

"What's that?" she asked, pointing to my right pocket. "Let me see it."

"It's my asthma rescue inhaler," I said as I showed it to her.

"Okay, but next time put it in a clear ziplock bag so it can be scanned with your other stuff."

Finally I was told I'd have to wait for the director of the Faith and Character Program, who would escort me to the unit where I'd be teaching a parenting class for mothers.

Good grief, I thought, *if it takes thirty minutes every time to get through security before I even start, plus the two hours they've allotted for the class, I'm in for a long day.*

Welcome to maximum-security prison.

—

As I stood waiting in Central Control, a memory flooded in of an afternoon years before when I had done a phone interview with an Oregon woman for a book I was writing entitled *When Mothers Pray.* Valerie was the leader of a Moms in Prayer group in her community, and I'd been told she had a really good story to share.

However, it wasn't the story I thought she'd tell me: how much her children and her friends' kids were blessed by their weekly prayer meeting at her home or all the answered prayers they'd seen. Instead, she told me about her experiences going every week into Salem

Penitentiary, a women's prison near the city where she lived, to lead a prayer group for the mothers.

My heart was suddenly stirred as Valerie described what happened the first night the mothers joined her to pray for their children. She walked them through praise, confession, and thanksgiving and then asked them what they were most concerned about for their kids that they wanted to pray about. Then Valerie prayed a scripture for each of their children, and they prayed it aloud with her, putting their child's name in the verse and lifting up the needs of each of their children.

One by one tears began to flow down the faces of the moms as they realized that here was someone, a mother like them, who cared enough to pray for their kids, and that they could actually *do* something for their children—something that could make a difference in their lives—even while they were separated by prison bars and razor wire.

Just like other moms, these women worried about their children. Some expressed how they were concerned about their kids' living situations while they were locked up. Others said they agonized about not being able to hug them, tuck them into bed, or provide the clothes and material things their children needed. Some of the children were struggling in school and there was no one to help them. Many of the mothers never got to see their children because they lived too far away. One young woman told the group she was about to deliver her first baby and knew that after a few days in the hospital, she'd have to give her infant up and return to prison alone.

"You may not be able to take your children on your lap and provide the things they need," Valerie told the mothers. "But even here in prison you have the ability to pray for your child—and that's the most important thing you can do." For the first time in many years, these women had hope that they could positively influence their children's lives.

A few minutes after we got off the phone, I was on my knees asking God to open the doors for me to go into a prison to teach and inspire mothers to pray for their children. I longed to instill that kind of hope in moms who were separated from their children.

And I wanted to start *soon*.

As I continued to pray about this idea and ask around, I was told that Prison Fellowship, a national ministry to incarcerated people, might be interested in partnering with me or letting me come under their umbrella. But when I called and talked to representatives in the national office, they said unless I already had an established ministry, they wouldn't be able to work with me.

I was not part of a larger ministry.

I was just one person.

Over the next few years, although I asked other people, including a woman who taught Bible studies at the county jail and another who knew someone at her church who ministered in prison, and followed up on these leads, not a single door opened.

Not to be dissuaded, I called a downtown church that held worship services at prisons in Oklahoma, but when the pastor heard what I had in mind, he said prayer groups for mothers wasn't what they were focusing on. Their purpose was evangelism.

"Lord, I'd really like to go share with moms in prison about how powerful prayer is and teach them to strategically and hopefully pray for their children," I'd pray periodically.

Yet it wasn't in the next months or year that this prayer was answered. In fact, as the years went by, I put that request on the shelf. I figured if God wanted me to go, He was well able to show the way.

One early morning in 2008, I was reading the newspaper and was struck by an article that reported that my state—Oklahoma—had more incarcerated women per capita than any other state in the nation.[3] And 85 percent of the women leave behind children.[4]

The statistics in the article, based on research by a leading sociology research professor at the University of Oklahoma, described with specific data the devastation in the lives of the children whose mothers were incarcerated, often for years at a time for nonviolent charges. From stigma and shame to worry and anxiety about their moms, many children suffered from the trauma of being at the scene when their moms were arrested. Being separated from their moms led to depression, sadness, and acting out at school because of the emotional turmoil they experienced, the research said.

These children had done no wrong and committed no crime. But they were suffering immeasurably.

I had to do something for them. I longed to make a difference in their lives. I knew each one of these children was valuable and without any intervention or help, many would end up on the pathway to prison like their parents. Since I was a former educator and had spoken at many parent conferences, I knew that one of the main ways to start helping the children was to teach their moms how to be better parents and how to rebuild their relationship with their kids even from behind bars.

Could I recruit others to go with me? Join up with some group already serving inside the prison?

I sensed God didn't want me to wait for that but that He wanted *me* to go teach moms in prison. There were a few major obstacles, however: I'd never set foot in a prison or jail before, I didn't have a curriculum yet, and all my previous attempts to pursue an outreach to women in prison had led to closed doors.

But once again I prayed that dangerous prayer: "Lord, I want to go teach and help moms in prison."

Later that very day I ran into Cynthia, a friend I hadn't seen for a number of years. We had both read the article in the *Oklahoman* newspaper and began talking about the plight of the children of imprisoned mothers.

"Cynthia, for a long time I've wanted to go into prison and teach moms how to pray for their children, how to reconnect with and encourage them even from behind bars," I told her. "Do you know how I'd go about it?"

"Well, I started teaching a Bible study at Mabel Bassett Correctional Center a few months ago for a group that's been going there for eighteen years. I got badged, and I think you can, too," she said.

I had no idea what "badged" meant. But I asked her what to do.

"First you complete an application; I've got one right here, so I'll copy and send it to you. Just fill it out and mail it to the Department of Corrections volunteer department. After they do a background check on you, you can get approved and go for a day of training. You need to be part of a group or church that's already approved. And you'll have to be on a waiting list; so many churches want to minister in prisons, it can take up to a year or more to get in."

From that point, things progressed quickly even though I wasn't already part of an organized ministry or church serving inside the prison system in our state. I sent in my volunteer application the next day, was approved within a month, and was invited to a one-day volunteer training session.

On that day of training a few months later, I sat in a big room filled with people eager to volunteer. And during a break I talked with the director of the Faith and Character Program at the maximum-security women's prison an hour away. She was one of our trainers. She was curious because most of the other people at that training session were from churches, signing up to go to prisons to lead Bible studies or worship services.

"But you're not with anybody. What are you wanting to do at Mabel Bassett?" she asked.

I shared my concepts for a relational parenting and prayer class to equip the mothers to give their kids the best gift any mom can, even from behind bars—the gift of their prayers, and to give them solid parenting methods, ways to encourage their children, and creative ways to reconnect with their kids and show them they loved them.

"That's a lot you want to do! But you're right on target. Did you know that the mothers' deepest pain is what they've done to their children and that they are separated from them? Their biggest need is to *do something* for their kids that makes a real difference," she responded.

As we talked a little more, she ended our conversation with, "When do you want to start?"

So I went to prison a few weeks later for the tour and orientation the program director took me through.

On the day of the first class, after going through the hassle of the security process, I found myself in the unit or "pod" where the women lived. Encircling the table area where I sat waiting were two hundred women's prison cells, upstairs and down all around the perimeter of the building. When the guard gave the word and the concrete doors opened, the women streamed into the communal area and some took their seats around me.

As I sat there with twenty-five eager mothers, somehow I knew that I was prepared for this and supposed to be here. I didn't feel a bit bit of fear or anxiety, only calm. And I knew I wasn't taking Jesus into Mabel Bassett maximum-security prison—He was already there, working among the women.

He just wanted me to join Him.

God hadn't forgotten my prayer uttered the same day I heard Valerie's story about her prison prayer group for moms many years before. In fact, He'd inspired it and had a right time for me to walk through that razor-wire-covered entrance and the numerous concrete doors of the prison I had to go through to get to these mothers.

That didn't mean my path would be problem-free—far from it! Some days, right in the middle of the two-hour class, the guard would blow a whistle for no reason and make all the women go back into their units. The doors would lock automatically, and I had to sit there waiting until the guard decided he was going to let them out. Other days, moms had to leave to stand in the medication line and get their antidepressants or anxiety meds.

It won't necessarily be easy when the Lord answers your dangerous prayer. But He promises to *be with us*, and He always was and is.

He was with me on the day when a young mother burst into tears, missing her three-year-old girl. He was with me on the day when I had an asthma attack and helped me get special permission to bring in medication, my rescue inhaler, and a bottle of water. He was with me when I felt inadequate and didn't think I had much to share. (I wrote the lessons for the mothers' class week by week and sometimes thought I might run out of ideas. But I never did.)

For most of the next two years I drove the hour to the prison and an hour back to teach the parenting class on Tuesday mornings. At first I went by myself until a few months later when God provided two women who wanted to go along and help when their schedules permitted.

After teaching about 380 mothers over the next two years, I discovered a great need that wasn't being addressed: the majority of the children rarely, if ever, get to see their mothers who were behind bars.

They don't get to look in their moms' eyes and see that they are loved. The kids don't get to be with their moms on Mother's Day like other children are. They don't get to be together making cookies at Christmastime with their mothers or even have a visit and a hug.

Most of these kids feel forgotten and left behind. And the majority of caregivers to these kids live too far away to drive to the prison and don't have gas money to bring them to visit their moms.

While the mothers showed me their children's pictures, sometimes they wept as they said how long it had been since they had gotten to see them or hug them. "I haven't seen my four children since I was in county jail three years ago," one said.

"My mom had to move back to New Mexico and can't bring the kids to visit because it's too far. I haven't seen them in four years," said another.

Slowly, an idea took shape, and God provided faithful people to help bring it to fruition: to find a way for children to get to see their imprisoned mothers.

—

Fast-forward about twelve months later. Through the windows of the chapel building, I see the rows and rows of silver razor wire and thick concrete walls surrounding the building in which our volunteer team is working. Long tables are filled with books, *Guess How Much I Love You*, *Love You Forever*, *Frozen*, and *You Are My Wish Come True*, along with sports books for boys, teen chapter books for girls, board books for babies, and scores of great children's stories for every age.

Twenty mothers are lined up to address their envelopes to their children and pick out the book they're going to read them while being videotaped. Fifteen more moms gather in chairs arranged in a circle as I begin to coach them on how to share a message that will encourage and comfort their children. All day long, the mothers keep coming in, eager to fill their children's emotional tanks with all the love in their hearts. By the end of the day, I and other volunteers on our team will have signed in, coached, and filmed fifty moms' Christmas messages to their kids.

I tell them, "We can't send you home for Christmas, but we can send you home via this video you're going to record that we will mail to your children with the book you read. Share a happy story with them. Tell them specific things you're proud of and how much you miss them. Say a bedtime prayer with them after you read the book—and don't forget to say 'Merry Christmas!' " I also encourage the moms about the power of praying for their children and provide a card with blessings for each day of the week they can pray if they'd like to take it. Hundreds of parents have eagerly taken and used these.

After all the mothers are coached and ready to record their message, Lynda, a reading specialist, teaches them how to hold the book up and read in such an engaging way, their children will want to read along each day. Then I follow Brandy, one of the women who is doing a Message from Mom for the first time, into one of the two filming rooms.

Brandy gets the microphone clicked on her shirt lapel and sits in the chair with a bright Christmas backdrop behind her. She's nervous, but she's been waiting for this opportunity for two months, so she takes a few deep breaths and begins:

"Hi, Brittany. Hi, Jason. Hi, Baby Jack and Karly. Merry Christmas! It's Mommy. I miss you so much. I keep your pictures right by my bed, and I look at them first thing in the morning and at night when I pray for you. I want you to know that Mommy is safe, and I am working to become a better mother. And kids, this is not your fault that we're separated. I made mistakes that brought me here, but I'm doing better. I'm working in the chapel office and have started taking college classes so when I get out I can get a good job and support you."

As she continues her message, Brandy sings "Happy Birthday" to one of her children and wipes a tear away. Then she introduces the book she's going to read. "I picked out this book for you because I know you love Dr. Seuss and I do, too. So let's read together now, and then every night when you go to bed, you can put in the DVD, get out your book, and we can have a bedtime story."

The moms can't leave the prison yard, but their faces are seen by their children day after day on the DVDs that our volunteers burn from the video camera's memory card. The moms remain behind bars, but their voices can be heard by their kids anytime they want to put the DVD in and get out their book to read along.

Our nonprofit, Oklahoma Messages Project, adopted this program from Virginia founder Carolyn LeCroy to serve the children, parents, and families affected by incarceration.[5] Since we launched this project in May 2011, our dedicated volunteers have served over 3,500 children in the state, bringing hope and a great sense of love to the kids, along with hope to their moms and dads. The children who receive these special message packages are less sad and worried about their parents, and they get more interested in school and reading.

What began as a simple yet dangerous prayer led to a project that—with volunteers and donors who give their time and funds—is making a huge difference in the lives of thousands of precious children and their families.

Chapter Two

BREAK MY HEART

Open up my eyes to the things unseen.
Show me how to love like you have loved me.
Break my heart for what breaks yours.
BROOKE FRASER

Honking horns and the roar of traffic on the loop circling inner-city San Antonio created a cacophony of noise as exhaust hung like a shroud over Holmes High School. The pride and despair that warred in the lives of the students and families revealed itself in the ongoing fight between graffiti and paint on the building. On the first day of ninth grade, fourteen-year-old Matthew Singleton's pale skin was a sharp contrast to the multicultural student body.

The year before, he'd attended a middle school where most students were not very different from him. He was happy to be going to Holmes High School; his mom had taught there for years, and he'd even gone to preschool there when he was little.

However, people at his church didn't think it was a good choice. The words of one of the Christian schoolteachers—who taught at the school operated by his church—had circled his mind ever since she said them: "Matthew, I hope you're *not* going to public school next year," she'd warned. "It's a very dangerous place."

Later, at a potluck dinner before youth group, a parent said, "Matthew, I heard you were going to the public school where your mother teaches. It's one thing to be an adult there—a person who is a strong and mature Christian—but it's full of bad influences that can get a young teenager like you on the wrong track. You shouldn't go there."

The majority of children and teens in their church attended the Christian school or were homeschooled, so people didn't understand why the Singleton kids were being sent to an inner-city public school all the way across town from the church. They didn't agree with his family's commitment to public schools—especially this one—and tried to convince them to change their minds. Like it or not, his parents were convinced that he and his sister should be there as a light to the other students.

Just keep to yourself and don't get into trouble, Matthew thought as he fought his way through the milling mass of students to get in the front door of the school. Looking up, he faced a wall of unfamiliar faces. *Oh boy. . .*

When it had first opened years before, Holmes High School had been a suburban school in a very desirable neighborhood. Each of the three buildings were built in a circle and topped with a lighted spire that could be seen for miles around. In fact, the architecture was so unique that it attracted national attention.

Now that spire stood as a beacon over pool halls, a payday advance check-cashing racket, a bar, and small family-run taco shops that were right across the street from the high school. While Matthew's parents wanted him to be like the light on that spire, all he wanted to do was blend into the crowd and not do anything bad.

As he walked in the big foyer, Matthew brought with him a stereotype in his mind of what an inner-city school in an economically depressed area would be like. And the gang affiliations. . .he anticipated all the dangers he'd been warned about. He did face some challenges being a white kid among predominantly Hispanic and African American students. But while some of the kids had gang affiliations, the "code" was that gangs didn't come to school. Occasionally there were fights on campus, but they weren't gang related.

In spite of his preconceived ideas about what it would be like attending Holmes High School, he found many good people and was surprised by the grace, kindness, and friendliness at the school, even from folks who weren't church people. He saw grace right in the midst of the poverty, troubled families, and deteriorating neighborhood.

He faced peer pressure, but about the same degree of peer pressure for social decisions that students in any public school would face. His parents had prepared him and his sister ahead of time with the idea that they were there to inspire and lead.

The longer he was at Holmes High School, the more Matthew's thinking was turned upside down because he was forming great friendships with guys from extreme situations and abusive homes. Many didn't know their fathers, and most lived in poverty with their moms, who worked two or three jobs. Many lived in chaos at home or were on their own most of the time.

One of his friends on the football team was left homeless when his mom died of AIDS and his dad was serving a long sentence in prison. Another family of a football player said, "Come live with us."

These people weren't your standard evangelical Protestant Christians like Matthew had known growing up. But he was often struck by the richness of the community, the acts of neighborly love. It began to raise more questions in his mind about what God meant the church in the world to be and what his role was as a believer.

At the same time, on Sundays he still heard from well-meaning church people, "Going to public school is bad for you. . . . There are teens there doing bad things. . . . Public school is the wrong place to be for a Christian, and you shouldn't be going to that high school."

So at first Matt thought his job was to be good and not do bad things or get in trouble. *Punch your ticket for heaven. Be safe. Don't put yourself in positions where something bad could happen. Don't be dangerous or risky.*

He'd led the "See You at the Pole" prayer event in September, and people knew he went to church. But that's where it ended. His way of interacting with other kids had been a smile and a pat on the back. *It's cool—everything's good as long as I'm good and don't have to worry about you.*

In the summer before his junior year, however, Matthew attended a youth conference in California, where he heard people talking about who Jesus was as portrayed in the Gospels. As he and his youth pastor talked about what they'd heard, he told Matthew that his mission field was his high school.

But Matthew knew that if Holmes High was going to be his mission field, he'd have to become a lot more compassionate about his friends' struggles. That he couldn't be content with shallow relationships because Jesus interacted with others at a deep level. Jesus was deeply impacted by people, particularly those who were broken or struggling, and Matthew knew his responses to people didn't match up with that.

There were plenty of broken, struggling kids around him. But when friends told him something bad had just happened to them, he hadn't felt any personal obligation or involvement. Instead, he'd thought, *Wow, crazy. That's awful.* It was like a movie where you could observe a scene and then smile and walk out. Matthew wasn't cold; he wanted to be a light. But he didn't think anything the guys at school were going through was related to him. He might say, "I'll pray for you," in passing, but he wasn't involved.

But he began to think, *If I'm really going to have faith, if Jesus is going to be the center of my life, if this is going to be my mission field, then I need to address this issue.*

That's when Matthew prayed the dangerous prayer that changed everything: "God, break my heart for people."

It was a simple prayer, very close to "Break my heart with the things that break Your heart," because God *loves people*—especially young people like those at Matthew's school who were broken, poor, and wounded—so much "that he gave his one and only Son, that whoever believes in him shall not perish but have eternal life" (John 3:16 NIV).

But it was also a bit of a scary prayer, especially for a young intellectual-type Christian like Matthew. *Okay, Lord, if this faith thing is real, then I've got to be all in. But I have this issue: I don't respond like Jesus would.*

As soon as he prayed that prayer, he knew he had no

idea how to start acting compassionately.

"Break my heart for people, God," he prayed again. "Let me not just feel sorry for them."

Praying that dangerous prayer was a turning point for Matthew. Almost immediately, so much changed. Most of all and first of all, *he changed*, for in those moments of prayer, he experienced an encounter with the living God. God's Spirit began transforming him and the way he saw people and the world as a result of his prayer, "Break my heart for people."

Now when he heard a friend at school share about a bad situation at home, his heart was softened and broken for the guy. He was filled with empathy. He sat next to friends when they were going through something hard and really listened.

He wasn't trained in compassion and hadn't gone to a seminar on the subject. Yet now he just naturally wanted to be there for those who were hurting. He went from having just casual friendships and being a buddy to the other football players to investing in their lives, helping them in any way he could, having them over for dinner, and doing life with them.

It was like he was now *in* the roller coaster with them instead of just watching them ride the roller coaster.

After football games, he often said to friends and players who didn't have fathers, "Hey, you need to come over to my house, have dinner with us, be around my dad, because he'd love to hear all about the plays you made at the football game. Come over and hang out with my family."

For the rest of high school, kids were always at Matthew's home, eating and talking around the table, watching sports with his dad, sharing their stories of their best plays, their struggles, their relationships, and their studies. His parents attended their games, concerts, plays. . .and the kids loved to hear his parents commend them afterward.

When Matthew signed up to go to camp in the summer, he invited other guys: "Hey, I'm going to youth camp. Wanna go? Let me find a way to raise money so you guys can go." And he always did. Some of those very people at the church who had warned him to stay away from the public high school even helped.

He still heard the church world saying to be safe, don't do anything risky or dangerous. But he was having raw, real-world experiences. He was involved with real people who were going through difficult situations and laying their problems out there. They couldn't hide them or put a suit on them to make them look better.

"When you go over to a buddy's house and his bed is a mattress on the floor and he says, 'I hate cockroaches because they crawl all over me at night; when I wake up in the middle of the night, they're on my face,' and yet he's hopeful and hungry for conversations about faith that aren't like a Sunday school conversation but real questions about God, there's just a big contrast," Matthew said.

"I saw his urgency about God, his wanting to talk about things of faith, and I didn't see that urgency in friends at church or even in myself. Once you really hear someone's story and you've been impacted, you can't *not* help do something. But I've found you have to be aware, broken, and open to hear their stories."

After two more years of high school, Matthew attended Baylor University, receiving a BA in journalism and English, and a master's in education curriculum and instruction. The moment he stepped on the campus as a freshman, he knew he wanted to be a teacher—and not for a private school or upper-crust suburban high school like he could easily qualify for.

No, he wanted to be a teacher for his alma mater, Holmes High School, in all its poverty and despair, pride and hope—because his heart had been broken for kids in that community.

That's why he now goes to work every day as a teacher and head of the journalism department, to bring a little piece of who Jesus is into his students' lives.

"I've got skin in the game with them. I always tell my kids on the first day of school, 'I don't know you right now, but I want to tell you I love you. You don't have to believe me. My job, besides being an excellent teacher and helping you learn all you can, is to prove it to you throughout the year.'

"And when they graduate," Matthew added, "they know it's not the end of our relationship. I want them all to know I'll be here, and forever, anytime, no matter what—you have someone in your corner who has your back. Ironically, the biggest rascals who gave me and all the teachers the most trouble are the ones who come back first."

Matthew, the friend who slept on the cockroach-ridden floor, and a few other guys from his high school started a home church in San Antonio called re:church 210. That's the area code of the community, because they look at Holmes High School and the surrounding neighborhoods as their parish. Their house church's youth group is led by his sister, Annie, and her husband, along with another couple.

Every week they take the teens out to dinner and pick up the tab. They love on them, talk about everything they're interested in, answer their questions about God, and along with Matthew, help them apply for scholarships to college. Their church has no paid staff or building, so all the money given goes to help kids and families in the community. They buy coats and donate them to the school to help put warm jackets on the backs of kids who don't have them. They provide meals for kids who otherwise wouldn't have food on the weekends.

All that grew out of a high school student praying a dangerous prayer for God to break his heart for people. As Matthew's heart has been shaped by God's love, he's committed himself to loving others—wherever and whoever they might be—instead of asking for a smooth and easy road.

Chapter Three

WHATEVER YOU NEED TO DO, GOD, BRING HER BACK TO YOU!

If you do not have an ongoing conversation with the Holy Spirit, you will become a paranoid mother whose legalism does not allow her children to face the giants God means for them to face.
DANNAH GRESH

Marlae sat by the phone rubbing her forehead, eyes closed in desperate prayer for her teenage daughter. It was pitch dark outside, and she and her husband, Dave, didn't know where Michelle was. After a shouting match, Michelle's anger spiraled out of control. She'd rushed through the front door and taken off running down the street, yelling that she was *never* coming back. She wasn't in a good place mentally or emotionally, and her parents were terrified about where she could be alone at night. Beside herself with worry, Marlae felt her stomach tie in knots when she thought about the possibilities.

Only a few nights before, Marlae had been sitting on their downstairs steps off the kitchen, sobbing uncontrollably. She felt beat up and abused. Michelle had started losing her temper more than usual. Knowing some drama is normal for teenage girls, Marlae tried to be understanding and keep communication open in the beginning. But that night Michelle's loud screaming of mean, hurtful words pierced not only her ears but also her heart as she took all her anger out on her mother.

"You don't understand anything! You don't know what it's like! You're a horrible mother!" Michelle blamed her mom for her misery and resented her even while she tore her mother apart.

Mornings were the hardest times. It was a challenge just to get her unhappy oldest child out the door to school. Many times she'd feed her kids breakfast, get all three of them out the door, and then sink into the couch and have a good sob. Then she went to Michelle's room and knelt by the bed praying for her.

What happened to my quiet, pretty girl who gave her life to Christ when she was young? she thought as she waited to hear from Dave the night Michelle ran away. He'd run into the night with his flashlight, looking in ditches for their girl. Marlae stayed by the phone hoping, praying she'd get a call from someone who'd found her.

Who is this angry, sullen teenager? What's happened to our sweet, compassionate girl who had eyes and a heart that could light up a room, who was obedient and such a joy to me and our whole family?

Until recently.

Michelle had always made As in school and, for the most part, was a good kid who had a lot going for her. She came from a happy home with parents who loved God and their children dearly.

But the middle school years were difficult for Michelle. Boys called her horrible names and were just plain mean. She didn't have a good self-image anyway, but their verbal abuse just fed into her lack of confidence.

As a freshman, she was on the junior varsity volleyball team and had many friends. Yet as she became more and more depressed, the hole inside her became bigger and bigger. She was sullen, sad, and angry. Her mom took her to the doctor and she began taking antidepressants, but the medication didn't seem to help.

Michelle didn't know what to do with her dark emotions. It was like something was missing inside her. She had to find something to fill that hole.

She tried filling the hole with drinking, partying, skipping school, and boys. But those things never did the trick. That gaping hole stayed with her wherever she went, making her restless and sad. The escape and fun of the alcohol and parties always wore off, making the hole bigger and pulling her down fast and hard.

As she self-destructed on the inside, she gravitated to all the wrong friends. Her grades plummeted. She quit the volleyball team. She hated herself. Most of all, she was dragging her family down with her into a pit so deep she couldn't get herself out, and her parents had no idea what to do. Nothing they tried worked to help bring a turnaround.

Through those dark days of their daughter's rebellion in high school, Marlae prayed this dangerous prayer: "God, do *whatever You need to do* in her life to get her attention and cause her to realize she needs You *desperately*."

One afternoon Marlae was with her son at his piano lesson when she got a call from her husband at the piano teacher's house. One minute she was enjoying listening to their youngest child play the piano and thanking God that things had gone better that week. The next minute her husband was telling her that Michelle was in the hospital. Michelle had attempted to overdose on pills.

Their middle daughter had walked in on her sister while she was taking a large handful of pills. She got very scared and quickly called her best friend's mom who lived in the neighborhood. This mom tore over to their house and rushed Michelle to the emergency room.

By the time Marlae and her husband got there, Michelle was calmed down and thankful to be alive. They saw it as a big cry for help. The doctors would only release her from the hospital if they would take her to a mental health facility for evaluation. Late that night, they drove her to a psychiatric hospital. After asking her a battery of questions and evaluating her, the doctor said they could take her home.

What a failure I am as a mother. I can't keep my daughter safe—even from herself.

In spite of praying hundreds of prayers, standing on God's Word, and believing that even these hard things could be woven into their lives for good, she was scared for her girl who kept spiraling downward. But when she prayed weekly with the other mothers in her Moms in Prayer group, their prayers were a balm to her soul and brought hope to her deeply hurting heart. They were her lifeline. She'd leave with a renewed hope and belief that she served a God who specializes in brokenness and impossibilities.

Marlae knew she couldn't give up praying, and she didn't. Every Tuesday she put a love note on her kids' pillows. She told them she loved them and wrote out the verse that she'd prayed that week in her group. God gave her Isaiah 61:3, and she prayed it hundreds of times for her daughter and believed that no matter what, He was able to "bestow on [her] a crown of beauty instead of ashes, the oil of joy instead of mourning, and a garment of praise instead of a spirit of despair. [She] will be called [an oak] of righteousness, a planting of the LORD for the display of his splendor" (NIV).

Marlae had trouble sleeping at night and often felt exhausted. She was burdened for her other two children who were two and six years younger than Michelle, that they had to live in the disruptive, unhappy place their home had become. And she felt awful that she had so little attention to give them, though she tried her best.

She took Michelle to a counselor to try to get to the root of her problems and find a solution, but those sessions didn't seem to bring her back to any stability or happiness.

The situation continued to get worse. Finally, through much advice and prayer, Michelle's parents sent her to a family member's home to try to help her reconstruct the life she was destroying and to get her away from the bad influences that were pulling her down. That dangerous prayer that God would do *whatever He needed* to do in her life to get her attention and cause her to realize that she needed Him desperately led them to send her twenty-five hundred miles away to try to help her.

The day Marlae and her husband put Michelle on a direct flight across the country, they cried all the way home from the airport. Letting her go was excruciating. But now she was truly in God's hands and completely out of their hands. Marlae knew that all she had was prayer. . .and boy did she hang on to it and cling to God the whole summer her girl was gone.

Michelle hated her parents for sending her away and told them so. For several months, she was so angry she would barely talk to them. She was away from all she knew in a strange world. No friends, no car, and no parties or fun. One day that summer a switch turned on inside her head, and it dawned on her that she didn't have to live this way anymore. She realized she was the one choosing the next move, and she no longer wanted to feel the pain and agony she'd experienced for so many years.

When Marlae and her husband heard their daughter was opening up a little to spiritual things and had met a nice guy she was dating, hope bloomed like daffodils appearing after a long stretch of stormy rain. Before her senior year, they flew out to see her and enjoyed being together. They also sensed she wasn't strong or stable enough to come home. So instead of getting to experience senior year with Michelle, which Marlae had looked forward to for so long, they said good-bye. One by one the bricks that had formed a seemingly impenetrable wall of separation between them were coming down.

Michelle was enrolled in high school and was even taking some college classes for her senior year. She got a job and had a new boyfriend. They could tell by her voice on the phone that she was less angry and depressed. Her life was getting back on track.

Then one night the phone call came at 1:00 a.m., waking them out of a sound sleep: "Mom, Dad, I'm pregnant." When Marlae first heard those words, she almost fell apart, but she was able to respond in love and with a degree of calmness. Handing the phone to her husband, she was grateful she'd been learning more about God's grace *for her*. Her husband talked with Michelle and her fiancé that night about forgiveness and confession and promised their love and support. Only nineteen and twenty-one, the two were scared to death, but they were going to get married.

Marlae and Dave helped plan a small wedding and celebrated the birth of their precious first grandchild.

When the young couple struggled—and they struggled often—they supported them in specific ways. But in the midst of the problems they experienced, Marlae could see even this as an answer to her desperate prayer of "Do whatever You need to do, Lord. . . ."

Several years later, the young couple's marriage unraveled, and suddenly Michelle was a young single mom. But again Marlae began to see another answer to her dangerous prayer as she saw God replacing Michelle's stubbornness and strong will with the positive side of that temperament: a good work ethic, intentionality, and dependability. She did a great job as a young single mom juggling work and motherhood and all the demands it brought.

Then one day Michelle told her parents about a new young man in her life. The relationship sounded promising—until Marlae realized he was the very guy Michelle had dated and gotten in trouble with in high school.

Another disappointment. But with it came a lesson in second chances. As she prayed and prayed about the relationship, she felt God saying to her, "So, Marlae, I've just shown you a picture of My redeeming, love and power in your girl's life, and now you aren't giving this young man a similar second chance? You are really acting like this young man's life isn't redeemable, and you're holding him hostage to his past. Is that fair? Do you think that's how I see him? Don't you think I can redeem his life as well?"

Marlae can still picture the day she drove up to her daughter's house and saw the guy's car in the driveway.

He was working on something in the bedroom, and she sensed the Holy Spirit nudge her to go talk to him. Marlae humbly apologized for not accepting him.

"I hadn't believed that God could make all things new, and I give you my word that I am not going to walk toward the future by hanging on to the past with all its pain and bad memories. I give you my word that I'll pray for you and Michelle and trust God with your relationship."

One year later, the two were married.

At the wedding, he surprised his new five-year-old daughter (their granddaughter) by stopping the wedding ceremony and bending down to put a lovely necklace around her neck. As he smiled and gave her a hug, he told her he would do his very best to be a daddy figure in her life, to love her and help her grow in the best way he could.

There wasn't a dry eye in the place. As Marlae watched this newly married couple walk back down the aisle and out the door to the waiting car, God reminded her this was a picture of His grace once again.

Today, Michelle is a mother of two children and is grateful for a mom who never gave up on her, and who through all the dark times found ways to show her that she loved her and was continuing to pray, no matter what. No one knew that Michelle had saved every note that said "I love you" with verses her mom prayed each week. She's truly becoming "an oak of righteousness, a planting of the Lord for the display of His splendor". . .and she is shining brightly.

And like her mother did, she is praying for her daughter, who is now in middle school.

Chapter Four

LORD, SHOW ME THE WAY

*The mystery of seeking God is
that He is the One who finds you.*
KINGSLEY OPUWARI MANUEL

In the aftermath of 9/11, the smoke and ash that mushroomed from the Twin Towers and the Pentagon had spread across America in much the same way that the ashes of Auschwitz had once blocked the sun over Poland. Like the rest of America, Mona felt as though her heart had imploded as well. As people tried to make sense of the horror, she began to be asked to speak on behalf of her Muslim faith in the community she lived in. While she'd been honored to do so, she felt conflicted and inadequate.

After all, men—not women—were active in the Muslim religion. In addition, she was more of a cultural Muslim and didn't know the Qur'an at all. Although she'd been born in Kuwait and had lived in Saudi Arabia when she was young, before her family immigrated to the United States, she didn't speak or read Arabic.

Instead of accepting an arranged marriage her father was planning, at age twenty-one and out of college, Mona told him she wanted to marry an American. For this, she'd been disowned by her family.

There were three strikes against the couple: First, Stephen was *not* the arranged suitor. Second, he wasn't a Muslim. And third, he was an American—all huge no-no's. At first her father threatened not to attend the wedding. But because Mona and Steve agreed to be married by an imam in the Muslim way, her parents decided to come to the wedding.

It took almost three years to rebuild their relationship with her family. In 2001 she and her husband and their two little boys moved to Oklahoma. Suddenly, following the terrorist attacks in September 2011, while presenting talks to various groups, she felt she must study and know more about her faith.

I ought to read the Qur'an and learn about the beliefs of Islam. I've got to become a better Muslim, she thought. She enjoyed being a Muslim; being involved with any other religion had never entered her mind. But she'd never read the Qur'an for herself, and there was so much she didn't understand.

Each day as she opened the Qur'an and read, she ended up with more questions than she had started with. When she called her mom and told her she was having a hard time understanding it, her mother encouraged her, "Why don't you ask God, because He wrote it and His truth is in there?"

So Mona began to pray, "Lord, show me the way."

She prayed this many times and had almost reached the end of the holy book when fear prickled the back of her neck like a spider crawling into her hair. Closing the book, she covered her face with her hands. The words she'd read had confused her. Without intending to do so, she'd almost committed blasphemy. A good Muslim can't wonder why. The moment you question or doubt the Qur'an, you're no longer a Muslim.

Horrified at what she'd almost done, she prayed again, "Lord, show me the way."

Mona had no idea that she'd been praying the most dangerous prayer of her life. A prayer that would turn her world upside down. A prayer that could put her life in danger. A prayer that would alienate her parents, siblings, and extended family. A prayer that would change the course of her life—for eternity.

She didn't know what she was praying when she asked God to show her the way. Nor did she expect an answer. But the next day she heard three words like an echo in her head saying, *Go to church.*

"I almost laughed because I knew there was no way that God would tell *me* to go to church," Mona said. "My family was Muslim, and we didn't even go to the mosque except on rare occasions. It would have made perfect sense to me if I'd heard, *Go to mosque.*

"When I woke the next morning, the first thought in my mind was *Go to church.* That was strange because church wasn't on my radar, and I had no intention of becoming a Christian. I liked being Muslim."

When she went to bed that night, the last words that echoed through her mind were *Go to church.* Three very clear words she'd never thought of in her entire life.

But it didn't go away: every morning the first thought was *Go to church.* When she lay down at night to go to sleep, the last thought was *Go to church.*

The thought was so persistent Mona realized that it wasn't a suggestion—it was a command. However, she assumed the command wasn't for her. It was for her husband, Stephen. Just like she was a cultural Muslim, Stephen was a cultural Christian. He was raised in a Christian culture, but he didn't grow up going to church with his family.

That evening when Stephen got home from work, Mona said, "I think God wants you to go to church."

"Absolutely not."

"But Stephen. . ."

"If God wanted me to go to church, He'd tell me." Conversation closed.

Going back to God that night before bed, Mona prayed, "God, show me the way."

Go to church, she heard.

Stephen didn't seem interested, so now Mona wondered if the words about going to church were meant for her children. Not long afterward, a woman she knew from her son's YMCA baseball team said, "Mona, are your kids going to vacation Bible school this year?"

"What is *that?*"

"Honestly? You don't know what that is? You bring your kids to church for a week; they have fun, get a free T-shirt, and learn about God."

That must be it! That's what I'm supposed to do! Happy to be obedient to God, Mona, expecting their third child, enrolled her sons, Jacob and Joshua, for vacation Bible school at the church where her friend's children went. On Friday when she went to pick up her boys, she met the pastor. And he invited her and her husband to come on Sunday.

"I'm not interested in coming to church," Mona replied, but then she lied and told him her husband was.

That night at dinnertime, she said, "Hey, Steve, the pastor at First Pres personally invited you to come to church on Sunday."

"What?!" he exclaimed. "Where'd you meet the minister?"

"I met him at the church. The kids were at VBS there this week."

"What?! They've been going this whole week?" He threw down his napkin, his eyes flashed and jaw clenched. When Mona saw her husband was mad, she began to cry.

"Well, God's been saying, 'Go to church,' and I'm not going so you'll have to," she said, wiping her tears with her hand. "In our culture, Stephen, pastors or imams are considered men of God. This pastor is a man of God, and he personally invited you."

"He doesn't mean it. He probably says that to everyone he meets."

"No, he really wants you to come," she urged.

"Oh, fine, if you want to play that game, you go with me. This Christian isn't going to church unless this Muslim does!"

On Sunday morning, the couple huddled in a dark corner of the sanctuary during the service and made a beeline home. But while they were at church, they saw an announcement that said the church was accepting new members, and Mona suggested that to her husband.

"You should become a member just for the sake of our children!"

"It's been over two decades since I've set foot in a church. You're lucky I went today. No, I won't become a member!" he said.

So Mona signed Stephen up for the new members' class and gave his work phone number and e-mail to the church office.

When he got home from work the next day, he said, "What have you done? They've got my e-mail and phone number! I can't be anonymous anymore!"

Tears flowed down Mona's face. "Stephen, it's not leaving. These words continue in my head every day: *Go to church.* I think God wants our children to be dedicated to Him, and this is the only way."

They had agreed that the children would be raised Christian because in Islam, the children are the husband's religion. "Okay, I'll go to the new members' class," he said reluctantly, "but only if you go with me. We can check it out, but you have to go."

For the first new members' class, Leo, the associate pastor, explained what the Trinity was. On the way home, Mona said, "All that talk about the Trinity; that was blasphemous to me as a Muslim. I would never want to go back to that class."

"We should go back to clarify what he meant," Stephen responded. Mona wasn't happy about that but agreed to go on the condition that he would *never ever* make her go again to the church.

The next Sunday when they got to class, they sat in a small group and Mona confessed to Ron, the leader, that she was a Muslim and not interested in being a Christian. Ron got Leo, the associate pastor, to come join their circle, because on that particular day, only two people showed up: Mona and Stephen.

Leo asked, "Why are you two here if no one wants to be here?"

"Look, I don't belong here. I'm a Muslim and don't

want to be a Christian," Mona told Leo. Both she and Stephen were in bad moods and didn't want to be there.

"Sometimes our spouses get us to do things that we really don't want to do," Leo told Stephen.

"Yeah, I know," Stephen answered.

"Wait, are you Muslim? Ron said you're Muslim. Are you?"

"No, I'm a Christian," Stephen answered.

"So who brought you to church?"

"She did," he said, pointing to his wife.

"Let me get this straight. Your Muslim wife brought you to church, and you don't want to be here?"

Leo was so confused, he asked the couple if they'd meet with him in his office on Tuesday. "This is too big to discuss today."

A few days later when they entered the pastor's office, Leo put out his hand and gave them both a warm handshake, welcoming them in. Shelves full of theology and counseling books lined the wall by his desk, but he didn't sit behind the desk. He came and sat with them in comfortable chairs.

After some conversation about their children and what Stephen did for a living, Leo asked Mona, "What are the five pillars of faith?"

"They are faith, prayer, supporting the needy, fasting during the month of Ramadan, and the pilgrimage to Mecca once in your life," Mona explained. "That's how you earn your way to heaven. But I've never been able to keep the Ramadan fast or to pray five times a day."

"Three out of five pillars does not get you to heaven,

right? You have to do everything?" Leo asked, and Mona agreed.

After he explained about Christ and His grace, he asked, "Why are you here—why did you come to church, Mona?"

"Because God told me."

"That's correct; that's God's Holy Spirit. Do you know why He told you?"

"Surely it's for my husband. That's why God wanted us to go to church," she answered.

"No, it's because God's grace is on you."

"I don't know what that means."

"Grace is unmerited, undeserved favor," Leo continued. "And it's on you. That's why you're here. He's calling you. He loves you. Here's the part about grace. It's offered to everyone, but not all listen, not all hear. Not all respond or are obedient. But you are here."

"Yes, I am."

"Do you know why?"

"Yes, there's an entire chapter in the Qur'an called Maryam, and it's about Jesus and about Mary, and I read that. Yet I just couldn't reconcile the differences between Jesus' amazing miracles as chronicled by the Qur'an and Muhammad's only miracle, the Qur'an itself. That was the source of my questions. That's when I asked God to show me the way."

In that moment she realized it as clear as day that when she'd asked God to show her the way, He did. He brought her right here.

Suddenly it felt like she'd been wearing a wrinkled

shirt, and someone took a big iron and smoothed out the wrinkles. In one instant all Mona's questions were answered and she was at complete peace.

"Do you believe that was God's voice calling you to church? That was the Holy Spirit, and His one job is to point to Christ," Leo said.

"I believe that."

"Then will you accept Christ Jesus as your Lord and Savior?"

"I do," Mona responded.

Her husband's very calm demeanor changed instantly as his face registered complete shock. He almost jumped in surprise as he turned to Mona, and couldn't comprehend his wife at all or what she'd just said. Though he didn't see it coming, he was in awe of the conversation between Mona and Leo because he had no idea she'd been struggling with her own beliefs about the Qur'an for the past three years.

The only thing he'd seen was Mona trying to read the Qur'an and to delve deeper into Islam. When she answered that she would take Christ as her Lord and Savior, it came out of the blue for him.

"Stephen, I've had so many questions. I didn't know what was true. I've been praying, 'Lord, show me the way,' for three years. And I've had this voice that won't leave me alone. I thought it was for someone else. But it's God calling me. I believe it's God's blessing on me."

What she soon discovered was that Stephen had been praying for three years. He, too, was struggling to know the truth and needed God's help to answer his sons' questions. Like the day that he and little Joshua had been driving by a local church in their neighborhood and Joshua said, "What's that building?"

"That's Santa Fe Presbyterian Church," Stephen had told him as he tried to explain the concept of church. His heart broke when he realized his son didn't even know what a church was. After that day, Stephen had felt guilty that he hadn't ever taken his kids to church. But he knew if he went on a journey of faith, Mona would get left behind, and it would cause a rift in their marriage. His wife wasn't budging from Islam. She was adamant. All he'd heard from her was, "I want to be a better Muslim. I don't believe I'm a good enough Muslim."

He was distraught and conflicted. *I can't do it. I can't go to church. I don't want to be a Christian because I will lose my wife. God forbid someone saw me at a church. It's out of the question,* Stephen thought. So he prayed that God would lead him because he felt at odds. He prayed God would overrule the fears that his wife wouldn't be involved in the spiritual part of his life. Stephen kept praying.

For three long years.

They had been on two separate train tracks, and God had those two paths converge in Leo's office that day. And in a moment, a lightbulb went on in both their minds and hearts. That day in Leo's office, Mona found that Christ was the answer to all her questions.

Leo led Mona through the sinner's prayer of confession and then led both husband and wife in prayer for the first time in their marriage.

"Now what?" she asked, eager to know what God wanted them to do.

"Now you can choose to be baptized as an outward sign of your inward expression of faith."

They decided to be baptized after Sarah was born. So in January 2007, they and their children were baptized together and continued on their new journey of faith.

Mona had had no idea what exactly she'd been praying for. But God answered in His amazing faithfulness. *"Okay,"* He seemed to say, *"I'll show you the way, the truth, and the life."*

She was elated that God had answered her prayer. She had found Jesus—the way, the truth, and the life.

Now came the dilemma of telling her parents she had become a Christian.

Ever since their baptism, Mona had prayed God would help her know how to tell her parents. They weren't going to understand this, especially her father. It had been so painful to be rejected and disowned the first time. She didn't know how she'd go through it again.

However, only two months later, a video was shown to the whole congregation. Mona learned that the man who had been called as senior minister had grown up in Saudi Arabia in an Islamic family and had become a Christian at Stanford University.

All the time she'd been praying, "Lord help me with this. I don't know what to do," God had been in the process of preparing the way for her.

After Mateen Elass, the new minister, arrived, he

and Mona began to dialogue about how to approach her parents in love and prayer.

Yet in spite of lots of prayer, she was very fearful and emotional. She knew what was going to happen. She knew she would no longer be her father's daughter.

On the day she picked up the phone to call her dad, she heard the Lord say, *"Don't worry about him. I am your true Father, and I have loved you since before you were born. I've always loved you and will always love you."*

Those words washed over Mona and the fear left. Calmly she explained her newfound faith to her father: "Dad, God led me to church, and this wasn't what I sought to do and it wasn't my plan. I was just trying to be a better Muslim. While I was trying to seek direction, the Lord led me to a church and straight to Jesus, and I believe this is God's will for me. I have to do it."

"This isn't happening. I can't listen to this!" he shouted. "When you got married I thought you were going to convert at that time. Do you understand what this means? We've disowned you for just marrying a Christian. Obviously you don't care about your family! You are very selfish and are going to do what you're going to do. There's no way our family can stand behind you on this decision."

His voice shaking with rage, he continued, "You are dead to me. You are not my daughter. Before we met you halfway. But not this time!"

The angrier he got, the more peaceful Mona became. "I'm sorry to hear it's come to this, Dad. But I love you and I will pray for you. I pray God will help you to see clearly."

"I don't need your prayers!" he said as he hung up.

Mona's parents didn't speak a word to her for over a year. Letters went unanswered. Phone calls weren't returned.

Her children often asked, "When will our grandparents come to see us? Why didn't they call for my birthday?"

Her mother finally called one day, saying she wanted to see her grandbaby, Sarah, their youngest child. Stephen was fearful that if Mona went home, some of her old Muslim friends in the community might harm her.

Stephen wasn't invited to her parents' home, so it took a lot of trust and both their prayers for Mona and her three children to fly to California that summer. Her mom set down the rules: "This visit is for the kids and us. This is not for you. So you will not talk about Christianity. And your dad isn't ready to speak to you. You will take a backseat."

As difficult as it was for Mona, that was the visit that started the restoration process. The strain was palpable. Her father wouldn't look at her if he walked by. He left the room if she was there. But he did interact with her children in a loving way.

The Lord showed her that it wasn't all about her and her feelings, however painful. *You have to walk the extra mile and be kind, compassionate, and forgiving. Be quiet and let Me work,* God told her. As a talkative young woman, Mona found that staying quiet wasn't easy.

Not until the second visit a year later was she able to make peace with her father through sharing the parable of the prodigal son. She asked for his forgiveness and told him she was that son who dishonored his father. "Forgive me for all the heartache I caused you," she asked.

Eight years later, the relationship with her family is still being restored. But through prayer and love, doors have opened. Mona has had an opportunity to share Christ with a sister, to give her oldest sister and nephew a Bible, and to pray with her younger sister.

Mona's father finally forgave her. On her last visit to her parents' home, he started asking about her and Stephen's faith and wanted to dialogue about their beliefs. At that same time, during a visit with her aunt after her aunt's husband had just died, she told Mona she didn't know what she believed anymore and that she felt Jesus had been calling her.

Her older cousin and Mona have also prayed together before. When she asked, "But how do I know God is listening?" Mona told her about the Good Shepherd and how the sheep know Him. "Have you heard Him call you?" she asked.

Her cousin started crying and said she had.

"Then you know His voice."

"You have no idea what peace that brings me," her cousin replied. "No one has been able to answer these questions as you have." Mona mailed her a Bible after she got back home to Oklahoma.

In unmistakable ways, God continues to work in her life and family—yet it all started with a dangerous prayer.

Chapter Five

A DESPERATE PRAYER

H.O.P.E.
Hold on.
Pain ends.

eigh Ann looked at the clock on the wall. The closer it got to 7:30, the faster her heart beat and the more her stomach churned, because that's when her husband would be home. It was the first day of his new job, and she didn't know what kind of mood he'd be in. She rushed into the kitchen and put her toddler in his high chair with a Cheerios snack and apple juice to keep him happy while she finished up the chicken enchiladas, green beans, and salad she was making. Her husband insisted on a big meal every night, even when she'd been working an eight-hour shift at the hospital emergency room.

As she drove home from work, her anxiety would rise. She worried about what was ahead, especially if traffic was moving slowly due to construction or an accident. If she was even five or ten minutes late, it would set him off into an angry tirade. She desperately wanted to make her husband happy. Yet as hard as she tried, she couldn't seem to please him.

The truth was, she never knew what he was going to do when she walked in the door. Would he give her a big hug and twirl her around, or would he get angry over something and lose it in a fit of anger?

Thoughts of how charming and affectionate he was in the early months of their relationship flowed through her mind. He'd seemed so crazy about her. And those eyes, she was so captivated by them. Her heart was calmed by his deep voice. Whenever they were together, Vincent made her feel good about herself. Sure, he was jealous and sometimes controlling when they were dating, but she didn't see those attributes as red flags. She just thought he acted that way because he really loved her.

And she wanted to get away from her unhappy home, where her father had made her feel like an unworthy loser. Where no matter how much she helped or tried to succeed in school, she could never do enough to please him.

In the beginning of their relationship, Vincent's love and attention filled the big hole in her heart. She'd found her Prince Charming who made her feel more special than she'd ever felt before. He told her she was beautiful and important. She knew he had some rough edges; he'd served time and even gotten arrested during their engagement. But she could polish those edges smooth. She was so in love with him, all she could see was their promising future and how happy they could be.

If I can just get him to believe that I love him and won't abandon him like all the other people in his growing-up years who were supposed to love him, then he can finally trust in my love. I believe that can happen.

More than anything, she just wanted to have a loving marriage and family. "He loves me; I know he does," she'd told her sister on the day of the ceremony.

But after the wedding, Vincent's control intensified. As time went on, he insisted she wear certain outfits and stop spending time with her friends. He wouldn't even let her talk on the phone with her sister. One Sunday when she wanted to go spend some time with her parents, he put his foot down.

"You have to choose me or choose your family," he told her. "You can't have both."

Leigh Ann chose her husband. And she grew more and more isolated. And afraid.

Even a smile from a stranger sent Vincent into a rage. Like the day they were sitting at a red light, and the guy in the car next to theirs smiled at Leigh Ann. He started yelling at her and calling her names, accusing her of being unfaithful. "I know you want to screw that guy! You're worthless!" he yelled as he smacked her bare arm with the back of his hand.

A year and a half into the marriage, Leigh Ann was forbidden to check the mail or answer the door or the telephone. She felt more and more like a prisoner in her own house.

As her husband's violence escalated, so did her fear. He went from kicking the wall or breaking something when he was mad to throwing things at her. Sure, he'd come back the next day and be loving and say he was sorry, but things only spiraled downward.

One night when she came home, he was angry about the stack of bills on the counter. He saw a $45.00 receipt from the store and yelled, "Why are you spending so much money?" When she tried to explain that little Vincent was out of diapers and needed some new T-shirts because he'd grown out of his little ones, and they needed some groceries, he flew into a rage. Grabbing Leigh Ann by her shoulders, he shook her hard. When she tried to wrestle out of his grip and leave the room, he shoved her against the wall and threw her down.

She didn't know what to do. She wasn't a Christian and didn't have a church to go to. She was too ashamed to go to her family. The words her mom had spoken long ago came back into her mind: "You made your bed. Now lie in it."

She had no friends to help her, and police were out of the question. Her husband had trained her *never* to trust the police and *never* to go to the police station about anything. Anyway, she knew if she called the police on a domestic violence complaint or asked for a restraining order, his parole would be revoked and he'd get locked up again.

"If I ever go back to prison, I'll make you pay for it," he'd threatened once. "I'll hunt you down and kill you. Or I'll have my friends do it."

A few days later, she was playing on the carpet with their toddler son while her husband was at work. The ball they were playing with rolled under the television set, and as she stooped down to get it, she saw a voice-activated tape recorder. She knew he'd bugged their phone, and now this?

She was trying to act in love and trust, walking around on eggshells trying not to make him mad. *No one else in the world has gone through anything like this. It's just me,* she thought, feeling so alone. *If I could just make him happy. . .* She'd worked so hard at being a good wife, and he still didn't trust her.

Soon after when she asked for a separation, he moved

into the extra bedroom but still kept tabs on her with cameras he'd installed.

One day she knocked on the door of his bedroom and slowly walked in. All of a sudden Vincent buried a big knife in the wall next to her head and said with a sinister look, "Don't you ever come into my room without permission."

She knew he always carried knives with him and had seen the thousands of holes in the garage walls. She'd heard the thuds from him throwing knives at the wall out there. He was obsessed with knives. But this was over the top.

Even though they were sleeping in different rooms, he followed her around, even spying on her during her shifts as a nurse in the ER to see if she was flirting with the doctors.

He was in a nasty mood anyway; he'd lost another job and now was accusing her of having a relationship with an ex-boyfriend from high school. While searching through old boxes of books in the garage, he'd come across a yellowed piece of paper with a note from the guy in one of her old college textbooks. He'd been calling the phone number on the paper all day to see who it was.

He was threatening her every day now. The words echoed in her mind even when he was gone, terrifying her. "If you cheat on me, I'll hunt you down and kill you and him. I'll kill your sister," he had snarled the night before while sitting on her chest with a knife to her throat.

That evening and many others when she got home from the hospital a little late because of a wreck on the highway that slowed traffic, he strip searched her because he thought she was sleeping with the ER doctor she worked with. Even as tears flowed down her cheeks, she put up with this humiliation because she knew if she refused, he'd be even more suspicious. He'd be sure she'd cheated and become even more violent.

Then for the first time, he threatened the unimaginable. "If you hurt me, if you think about leaving, I'll bring more pain than you could ever imagine. I'll kill your son."

That's strange. How could he say Vincent is my son and not ours? Despite her pleading cries for him to stop, the abuse continued until her husband finally fell asleep that night.

Okay, she thought later as she put ice on her bruises and wiped her tears. *I have to do what I can to protect my son because he's all that matters. What can I do?*

All she could think of was a gun. If he lost control and snapped, she could bring the gun out and say, "Okay, you have to leave now."

Then he'd go away and cool down and everything would be all right and her baby would be safe. That would make him switch from being out of control to realizing how bad the situation had gotten.

The following week he flipped out again. Sitting on top of her, he held a knife against her neck, slicing her like a surgeon with a sharp blade. "I'm going to rape you with this knife," he jeered. Terrified and bleeding, she screamed and struggled while he slashed her until she was bleeding all over.

"I'm going to make you watch as I kill our son, and that's the last thing you'll see, and then I'm going to kill you."

Calling for mama, their boy's whimpers turned into loud cries. She convinced him she needed to go into the nursery to calm the baby and rushed in, covered in blood. She grabbed the gun hidden up high in the closet, and when she got back, she pointed the gun at him and told him to leave.

He laughed and made fun of her. "That isn't real. Who are you kidding! You wouldn't know how to use it anyway."

She pointed the gun away from him and shot a hole in the wall. As he lunged at her, she knew no matter what, she couldn't let Vincent get the gun. If he did, he would kill her and kill their baby boy.

He wrestled for the gun, grabbing for it, fighting her for it.

Then it went off. It happened so fast. The gun went off a second time and he ran out the door.

Horrified, she ran outside and found her husband collapsed in the front yard. She called 911 and tried to give him CPR, but he was already gone. She froze, paralyzed. She'd never meant for this to happen. She loved Vincent; she just had to keep their baby safe.

Leigh Ann shot her husband in a desperate act of self-defense to protect her baby and herself. While the police were investigating, she spiraled into depression, nightmares, and PTSD symptoms. Suicidal thoughts threatened to overwhelm her. She couldn't eat, and it took every ounce of energy she could muster to take care of her son. At five foot five, she saw her weight slip down to ninety pounds.

She often called her late husband's family in the months that followed to ask if they wanted to see their grandson, little Vinny. But the answer she received was that it was too painful to have him around. Leigh Ann kept trying to get them to see him, just to care about him.

After the first few rejections in November, she prayed to an unknown God, "Please let Vincent's family care about his son and want to be a part of his life."

At Christmas she called and asked, "Would you like to have little Vinny over during the holiday?" When her mother-in-law answered no, she said, "Maybe you'd want to come over and go through your son's stuff and you can have whatever you'd like." His family wanted nothing to do with her or her little boy. She was devastated.

When she was first charged in December, she spent a couple of nights in jail and got out on bond. The following August, her bond was revoked and she had to leave her son with her sister while she went back behind bars.

But a few days after her arrest, her sister's husband, Ryan, collapsed and ended up in the ICU needing a liver transplant. So her sister worked it out for her son to stay with Vincent's sister. It was only supposed to be for a few days. But Rick got worse and worse. Leigh

Ann's sister couldn't care for Vinny, because she was too involved with caring for her seriously ill husband.

Leigh Ann tried many times to get Vincent's family to see her son during those months she was free, but in almost a year's time they ended up spending only two weekends with him and had a short visit at the park.

Leigh Ann so longed for his family to show some love to her son that she prayed again during this time for them to care about him. Though indicted for murder, all she wanted was for her husband's family to care about their grandson. And after her arrest, with her mother living in Vienna, Austria, and her brother-in-law dying of liver failure, Vincent's sister and husband said they could offer their home. So Leigh Ann's family let little Vinny stay with them.

When Leigh Ann went to jail, the family she had once prayed would show more interest in her son ended up suing her for custody. Her devastation and heartbreak were overwhelming. She lost temporary custody and couldn't even try to fight to win him back until after fourteen months in jail and a murder trial that ended without prison time. Vincent's family got very involved in little Vinny's life for several years, causing her tremendous emotional pain.

This was *not* what she thought was going to be the answer to her prayer. She had never imagined Vincent's family taking so much interest that they would steal him from her. Yet during those eighteen months behind bars, throughout her struggles and pain, she came to a transforming faith in Christ and experienced the first real freedom she'd ever known in her life. Eventually she got her son back, but it was a difficult and agonizing battle that lasted seven years and went all the way to the Supreme Court of Texas.

Yet in the end, her freedom through Christ and security in her salvation, as well as the peace and safety she found in having her son live with her, were all that mattered. Yes, her dangerous prayer brought intense pain, but the good that came from it far outweighed the negative.

Twenty years later, Leigh Ann and her college-aged son, Vincent Jr., have a loving relationship. She has been happily remarried for fourteen years. She and her husband have a thirteen-year-old son, and she has a twenty-eight-year-old stepson who is married with four daughters.

As a domestic abuse survivor, Leigh Ann courageously ministers to countless women through her speaking and her book, *In My Defense: An Unlikely Romance, a Deadly Gunshot, and a Young Widow's Road to Redemption*.[6] She offers tangible hope and resources to those struggling with physical, emotional, or sexual abuse and introduces them to a God who can heal a broken heart and life.

Chapter Six

MAKE YOURSELF REAL TO ME

She had the feeling that somehow, in the very far-off places, perhaps even in far-off ages, there would be a meaning found to all sorrow and an answer too fair and wonderful to be as yet understood.
HANNAH HURNARD

O God, if there is a God anywhere, You must make Yourself real to me. If You exist and are really what people describe You to be, You can't leave me like this," prayed Hannah, a young Englishwoman, as she knelt by her boardinghouse bed.

It was 1924 and the nineteen-year-old who prayed this dangerous prayer was in a deep pit of despair. She'd been raised in a strong Quaker home but hated church and had no relationship with God. Her parents loved the Bible and loved to worship. Hannah found both absolutely dismal.

Having struggled with disabling fears all her life and a profound stuttering problem, she was rejected, friendless, and left out of ordinary activities with other young people. By the time she turned nineteen, Hannah was so miserable and hopeless, she strongly considered suicide but was too afraid. She longed for the courage to end her life.

With each passing year, God seemed more unreal and unreachable to Hannah—and no amount of church services changed that.

Her father, who had prayed for his daughter her whole life, invited her to accompany him to a weeklong evangelistic Keswick convention in a nearby county. Despite her objections, he urged her to attend.

"Don't make me go, Father! I can't endure a whole week of being stuck in the tent all day and night and having to listen to sermons and hymns!"

Her father knew that from the time Hannah was young, she'd found church services dreary and depressing.

She didn't believe God was real. She hated Sundays and considered the Bible a dead book that held no meaning for her. What she loved was to be outside in nature hiking or riding her bicycle.

While she had refused to go to other spiritual weekends before, this time her father made an offer she couldn't refuse: if she'd go to only two meetings a day, one in the morning and one at night, she could spend most of her time hiking in the fields and riding her bicycle by the lakes and through the hills. And after the conference, father and daughter would take a vacation together.

Hannah agreed to go only for the outdoor times she was promised. Yet as the week of services dragged on, her mood grew darker. She became more depressed. Nothing preached resonated with her, and she couldn't stand being surrounded by hundreds of excited, worshipping Christians. It made her feel wretched and even farther away from God.

In the middle of one of the meetings, the speaker asked if there were any parents who would dedicate their children to the mission field. When her father put his hand on her head and prayed, she was mortified. She ran out of the tent as fast as she could and sped away on her bike to the boardinghouse where they were staying outside of town.

Falling on her knees beside the bed in desperation, she prayed, "O God, if there is a God anywhere, *You must make Yourself real to me*. If You exist and are really what these people describe You to be, You can't leave me like this."

A few minutes later, she picked up the Bible and turned to 1 Kings 18 to read the story of the standoff between Elijah and the Baal prophets. Hannah was struck by Elijah's challenge to the people of Israel: choose to submit to Baal or to the living God.

As she read how God caused fire to fall upon Elijah's sacrifice, it seemed that God wanted a sacrifice: her stammering tongue to use for His purpose.

Time stood still. *That's what I must do,* Hannah thought. *I must bring myself to the altar and yield my entire being and even my stammering tongue to God.*

But even while she was surrendering, a wave of fear ran through her. What if God would require her to stand before an audience and speak? That was her worst nightmare. She couldn't bear it. She wouldn't be able to get one word out. She'd be shamed. If God would put her through this kind of pain, how could she surrender fully to Him?

She reread the verses: "Then the fire of the LORD fell and consumed the burnt sacrifice, and the wood and the stones and the dust, and it licked up the water that was in the trench. Now when all the people saw it, they fell on their faces; and they said, 'The LORD, He is God! The LORD, He is God!'" (1 Kings 18:38–39 NKJV).

Suddenly a burst of light flooded into her dark, tormented mind. Jesus revealed Himself to her in such a tangible way that the sense of His presence never left Hannah the rest of her life. She expressed this encounter later in simple poetic words:

I have seen the face of Jesus,
Tell me naught of earth beside,
I have heard the voice of Jesus,
And my soul is satisfied.

When she got up from her knees, Hannah was a different person. For the first time in her life she felt joy. She felt secure; she was able to laugh and felt like clapping her hands and dancing for the sheer joy and happiness she experienced. From that moment on, she was just as sure that Christ stood right beside her as if she'd seen Him with her eyes. He loved her and had come to tell her that He wanted her and would use her, even with her stuttering problem.

For Hannah, the old life was gone; a new life had begun, as Paul describes in 2 Corinthians 5:17 (NIV): "If anyone is in Christ, the new creation has come: The old has gone, the new is here!" She'd been in church hundreds of times. She'd heard hundreds of sermons. She'd heard other people talk *about* God countless times.

But now she had seen the Lord for *herself.*

And that made all the difference.

It was like a miserable, stunted potted plant had suddenly been transplanted into a sunny, richly fertilized flower bed. As she described, "I was lifted out of the dreadful isolation of self-imprisonment and set down into the love of God."

Of course this nineteen-year-old needed to grow in character and maturity, but her whole purpose now was to serve God and develop what she called a "hearing heart," attentive to His every word and obedient to go *wherever* He guided her.

Hannah put herself on the altar that day at Keswick, just as she was—stammer, fears, and all. And as she grew spiritually, she allowed God to exchange her weaknesses for His strength, her inadequacies for His sufficiency. In the beginning of her walk with Christ, she still was terribly afraid of people, fearful of heights and the dark, of becoming ill and losing consciousness.

Worst of all, she was *terrified* of speaking in front of an audience because of her stutter. The first time she was asked to address a class at a Bible school, she was overwhelmed by physical panic. Her heart raced, her breathing was shallow, and her hands became clammy. She thought she would surely faint.

But instead of being deterred by the panic, she ignored it, opened her mouth, and began to speak. Suddenly it felt like Jesus was next to her, speaking through and for her. She communicated her message without a stammer or stutter.

As she wrote in the allegory *Hinds' Feet on High Places*:

> *"I love doing preposterous things," he [the Shepherd] replied. "Why, I don't know anything more exhilarating and delightful than turning weakness into strength, and fear into faith, and that which has been marred into perfection. If there is one thing more than another which I should enjoy doing at this moment it is turning a jellyfish*

into a mountain goat. That is my special work,"
he added with the light of a great joy in his face.
"Transforming things—to take Much-Afraid, for
instance, and to transform her into—" He broke off
and then went on laughingly. "Well, we shall see
later on what she finds herself transformed into."[7]

Surely the character Much-Afraid was fashioned after Hannah, a woman who was transformed into a woman of courage who overcame her fears and weaknesses to become a vessel God used for the rest of her life. The first day she spoke, and in the hundreds and hundreds of sermons and messages she later gave, every time she shared the good news of Christ's love in factories, missions, churches, and hospitals throughout the United Kingdom and in Jerusalem and Israel, those who heard Hannah remarked that God had given her a gift of speaking.

However, in regular conversation, she still stuttered as badly as she always had. Because of this affliction and her vocation as an evangelist, she was pressed into total dependence on God. She learned to walk by faith and always to go forward just as if she saw Jesus next to her, strengthening her to do whatever the assignment or task was. Because she knew He was.[8]

After serving for many years in Palestine, all missionaries, including Hannah, had to be evacuated due to impending war. They were furloughed to England for an extended time.

Hannah longed to return to her ministry to Jews

and Arabs, but every door was closed. The governments of both countries said it was impossible to return.

Then only a few weeks later she was offered a position as a housekeeper in a hospital in Palestine. That wasn't how Hannah envisioned getting back to the Middle East, so she refused. *I'm a terrible housekeeper and this can't be the way to resume my ministry in Palestine,* she thought. *I'm an evangelist, not a housecleaner! I preach the Gospel, not empty bedpans and clean sick people's rooms!*

To accept God's way of getting back to her ministry, she had to lay down her agenda and how she thought she would return. That wasn't an easy assignment.

Yet she had learned that there was nothing impossible with God. And that "when the Lord calls to some act of obedience which looks absurd, or doubtful, or even wrong, it is necessary to take the first step in obedience without paying any attention to doubts or fears. . . Always begin to obey, and after every new step ask if it is His will that we should keep going forward. He is faithful, and will check us if we have not really understood His mind. But it is hopeless to wait for further guidance or confirmation from the Lord until we have begun to obey in faith."[9] Obeying and walking in faith, laying down her will and loving with Christ's love—these are the lessons Hannah learned and passed on to readers in her books and messages.

When the hospital administrator, knowing clearly she had utterly no experience in housekeeping, sent letters of invitation, Hannah obeyed.

Three weeks later, she was on a flight back to the Holy

Land and became director of hospital housekeeping. There were times of hardship ahead. Danger, terrorism, snipers, and war awaited her. Yet joy and gratitude overshadowed everything else, even the learning curve of a job vastly different from any she'd ever done. Yet through this unlikely position, God gave her countless opportunities to minister to Jews and Arabs, even during wartime.

While the majority of Christians were cast out during that conflict and another war, Hannah was allowed to remain in the country due to her official hospital capacity.

While in the beginning she didn't like Jews, she grew to love them and developed many friendships. She ministered in Israel from 1932 to 1948. Though she hated housework, God gave her fulfillment in her position because it opened doors to people she otherwise never would have met. When she opened her mouth, the Lord gave her courage to share His love with others. Though in her early years she lived with despair and without hope, she wrote books such as *Hinds' Feet on High Places* and *The Hearing Heart* that have inspired millions of people.

I know because I was one of the people impacted by this book in my early adult recommitment to Christ. I, too, was a young woman struggling with my own fears and anxieties yet desiring to serve God fully. When I read Hurnard's classic allegory *Hinds' Feet on High Places*, the Lord used it in my life not only to give me a better understanding of my fears but to help free me of them as well.

After four years of working in the mission hospital,

Hannah began to travel from village to village sharing the Gospel in Jewish settlements. She knew many people in these remote places of Israel and Palestine would never be able to get to the hospital or to the mission to hear about Jesus. She felt God's call to go to them because her desire was always to reach the unreached. In her book *Wayfarer in the Land*, she tells the stories of her years of mission work among the Jewish settlers—failures as well as victories.

In her later years, Hannah Hurnard strayed away from what was considered authentic biblical truth and taught different, unorthodox philosophies for which she was criticized and ostracized from evangelical circles. Yet no one can mistake the fact that from that first day at the Keswick boardinghouse when God revealed Himself to Hannah and she gave Him her whole life, everything changed and she was set on the journey of a lifetime. Despite her unorthodox beliefs in old age, her books brought hope to countless people, and their influence remains today.

Chapter Seven

A PRAYER THAT CHANGED A LIFE

How glorious a truth it is that when we from our hearts murmur that prayer, "Oh, that someone would get me a drink of water from the well. . ." and behold, a tall, cool, crystal-clear glass of water appears before us. Cool and pure and good. This water eases our hot fevered souls and brings life and refreshment to our weary spirits—sick with their wandering, in need of forgiveness and renewal.
JIM McGUIGGAN

The woman wondered if it was safe to approach the well. She studied the man closely. He was fatigued; that much was clear. He had no bucket with him and he leaned against the rough stones as if the cool exterior might seep through to refresh his weary body. She adjusted the water pot, moving it so that it wouldn't press into the soft flesh of her shoulders. The man watched her as she walked, but he didn't stare at her like the other men in the city did. She blushed as shame crept from her heart and bled into her cheeks.

She narrowed her eyes, refusing to let the tears fall. She would not weep again. The losses in her life had reached with greedy fingers to take away everything she held dear. Five husbands. Taken from her by war, disease, death, her own unfaithfulness. . .it was simply too much. Who cared if the women turned aside when she passed them in the street? They hadn't lived her life. They didn't understand the agony of being alone. Perhaps if she could do it over again, she would. Perhaps if fate had been kinder to her, but there was no way to turn back time or change her life.

The man stood as she set the water pot on the ground. "Would you give me a drink of water?" he asked.[10] He brushed his hand across his dust-streaked brow. Wisps of his hair clung to his beard.

She stared at him, taking in the fine features, the inflection of his voice. He was a Jew! It wasn't unheard of for a Jewish man to enter Sychar, but most took extravagant measures to avoid this village. The Samaritans laughed at the pious Pharisees who traveled around the village, adding hard miles to their travel just so they could avoid coming in contact with them. A rabbi would rather be thirsty than violate his religious rules.

Jewish men weren't allowed to speak to a woman in public, much less a Samaritan woman. It was just one more insult piled on the heap of mutual loathing between the two races. It was rare for a Jewish man to talk to a Samaritan, but even more surprising that one would request a drink from someone like her.

"How come *you*, a Jew, are asking *me*, a Samaritan woman, for a drink?" she asked. She reasoned that his thirst must be greater than his pride under the hot noon sun, but she wanted to hear his answer nonetheless.

The man smiled. "If you knew the generosity of God and who I am, you would be asking *me* for a drink, and I would give you fresh, living water."

Why, the man doesn't even have a bucket, the woman thought. Jacob's well ran deep into the heart of the earth. Did he think he was capable of climbing into the well and drawing water from the depths and carrying it to the surface in the palms of his hands?

"How are you going to get this living water?" she asked. "Are you a better man than our ancestor Jacob, who dug this well and drank from it, he and his sons and livestock, and passed it down to us?" She turned to pick up the water pot. The sun had clearly taken its toll on this weary traveler.

"Everyone who drinks this water will get thirsty again and again. But anyone who drinks the water I give will never thirst—not ever. The water I give will be an artesian spring within, gushing fountains of endless life," the man said.

She turned. Who was this man who spoke with such authority and yet compassion? What was this water he was talking about? She had trudged to the same spot every day since she was old enough to carry the water pot. It was an endless chore, a daily routine. She needed water to drink, to wash the dust from her home, to bathe. If there were an artesian spring in the area, the word would have spread through the village overnight. Besides, there was no such thing as water that would quench a person's thirst so that they never needed another drink. She had listened to enough. Not only was he talking nonsense, but if her neighbors spied her talking to a strange man—a Jew at that—she would endure more gossip.

Dipping the water pot into the well, she let the rope slip gently through her hands. The water seeped into the pot and she quickly pulled it to the surface, the lean muscles in her arms responding to the familiar task. As she poured the cool water into a cup, she handed it to the man. He closed his eyes, drinking until every last drop was gone. She picked up the water pot and prepared to leave. The sun was hot and baking her skin, and in the far distance she saw a group of people approaching. It was time to go.

Yet she couldn't repress an urge to ask, "Sir, give me this water so I won't ever get thirsty, won't ever have to come back to this well again!"

As the man stared into her eyes, the woman was

gripped by his gaze and arrested within by his aura. His voice was gentle but resonated with a quiet, uncanny presence. "Go call your husband and then come back," he said.

"I have no husband," she replied.

"You've had five husbands, and the man you're living with now isn't even your husband. You spoke the truth there," he said. Heat flushed into her face as his words pierced her soul. Water splashed across her robes as she dropped the water pot on the ground. She barely noticed the cold water turning the dust to mud around her feet because the secrets of her heart had been revealed.

Had the rumors spread even to Galilee? Surely not! She quickly knelt and set the water pot upright. This man was like no other man on earth. Perhaps he was a prophet. How else would he know her past? She was angry with herself as the tears pressed against her eyelids. No! She would not cry. She stood and faced him.

"Sir, I perceive you are a prophet! So help me understand this paradox," she questioned, expressing her desire to know the proper way to approach God. "Our ancestors worshipped God at this mountain, but you Jews insist that Jerusalem is the only place for worship. Which is the right way?"

The man handed her the cup. "The time is coming—it has, in fact, come—when what you're called will not matter and where you go to worship will not matter. It's who you are and the way you live that count before God.

"The true approach to God is in Spirit and in truth. God is Spirit and He is seeking people who will worship from their hearts, worship based on the truth and through the Spirit," the man added.

It wasn't just the words, but the way he spoke them. As if he knew a secret that she did not, and his voice was so full of compassion. No one had ever spoken to her with such kindness. She stood silently, unsure of how to respond. *It does matter what you are called,* she thought. She was a Samaritan, despised by the Jews. She was a woman who was well known because of her association with men. She was judged by others daily, living under the scrutiny of disapproving looks and sideways glances.

She had resigned herself to her lot in life, yet God had a greater purpose for her than she could have imagined. Jesus walked into an area that was off-limits to Him as a Jew to make sure that she had a life-changing encounter.

She didn't understand everything He said, but she wanted to hear more. She had never heard anyone speak the way this man did. The prophet—or was He a teacher?—told her wonderful things. He said the Father was looking for those who were honest, those who would simply be themselves before Him in their worship. Perhaps there was a way to have a second chance, even if she had lost her way.

She smiled for the first time at the stranger. "I do know that the Messiah is coming," she said. "When He arrives, we'll get the whole story."

"I who speak to you am He," the man said. "You don't have to wait any longer or look any further."

She stepped back. Hope ignited, small flames that

dared to push past the hurt and shame that had branded her. One by one, the walls surrounding her heart began to crumble under the love that emanated from the stranger.

Suddenly she heard footsteps and instinctively moved back, shying away as several men called out to the man, calling Him Jesus. They looked at Him and then at her, amazed that He had been speaking with a woman, and a Samaritan woman at that. They didn't say what they were thinking, but their faces showed it. This she understood. It was familiar. But then she looked one last time at Jesus, and He smiled directly at her with a look of complete openness and acceptance. She knew unquestionably that this was no ordinary man.

She turned from the well and fled, forgetting the water pot as she rushed to the village. She couldn't wait to tell people about this man who knew about everything she'd ever done, a man who knew her inside and out, all the secrets, longings, and pain of her heart, and yet a man who would talk to her and take a drink of water from her hands. Jesus gave her His living water and said she'd never thirst again, and she was washed in the love and grace of God.

It was a day of transformation, a day of divine appointment for this unnamed woman. Jesus reached out and for the first time revealed Himself as the Messiah and as the Living Water, something He hadn't done publicly yet.

Someone once said that prayer is the encounter of God's thirst with ours. The woman's prayer, "Give me this water so I won't ever get thirsty," was a response of faith, even a dangerous prayer, because her people thought an exchange like this—between a Jew and a Samaritan—was unclean, taboo. In spite of that, this woman, who didn't need any more reasons to be further ostracized, asked Him for the living water. It may seem small to us, but the gesture of asking for a drink transcended several cultural boundaries—barriers that Jesus transcended as He sought a woman whom others despised and she responded. In fact, their conversation is the longest conversation recorded in the Bible between Christ and another individual.

What a breakthrough the woman experienced. She came with her water pot to draw water, but "she found a Well and had no further need of a water pot."[11] She had found the source, the Living Water, and thus left her everyday chore just as the disciples left their fishing nets, in order to spread the news of Jesus to all those in her town.

Though the Bible doesn't name her, it does recount how this very first missionary, a woman who had been despised in her town, spread the word about Jesus so enthusiastically that throngs of Samaritans came from surrounding areas to listen to Him. They even asked Him to stay in their town and listened to His teaching for two days, and they came to believe in Him as the Savior of the world.

Four years later when Philip the Evangelist came to preach in many of the villages of Samaria, he experienced a great gathering of souls, so much so that there was great joy in that city.

As Oswald Chambers said, "All that God has done for us is the mere threshold; He wants to get us to the place where we will be His witnesses and proclaim who Jesus is. Be rightly related to God, find your joy there, and out of you will flow rivers of living water. Be a centre for Jesus Christ to pour living water through."[12]

Chapter Eight

A NETWORK OF PRAYER

*Prayer lays hold of God's plan and becomes the link
between His will and its accomplishment on earth.
Amazing things happen, and we are given the privilege
of being the channels of the Holy Spirit's prayer.*
ELISABETH ELLIOT

Karen Covell sighed as they wrapped the last day of shooting on the documentary she had written and produced. Climbing into her car, she drove across Hollywood pondering what to cook for dinner for her husband and two sons. At home, she tossed the bills to one side and opened a letter addressed to her. Moments later, the color drained from her face. The letter fluttered to the floor.

Another letter spewing hatred and vile accusations.

Dropping onto the side of her bed, she stared into space. In 1977 she'd left Chicago for college, where her roommate was a Christian. When Karen gave her life to Christ her freshman year, she never imagined this. She had come to Hollywood to make a difference. Sure, she knew that after graduating with a theater and producing degree from USC, her faith might be problematic when she went to work in Hollywood. She knew that the culture of Hollywood was not a culture with open arms toward Christians. She'd expected some pushback.

But she'd been blindsided and saddened when the worst persecution, the most vitriolic hatred, spewed from professing Christians. This most recent hate letter had been one of many. Her name had been vaunted on a website listing people, including Karen and her husband, who claimed to be Christian but were not. Other sites warned people to stay away from her. All because she was a Christian working in Hollywood. Most church people thought that was an oxymoron. They didn't believe a real Christian would work in Hollywood, or that God would ask anyone to do that.

After almost twenty years in Hollywood, Karen

realized what that meant.

She couldn't win.

When she first moved to Hollywood in the early 1980s, the "Church" hated Hollywood. Christians had even built a housing development in the area a few years before because they wanted to have a Christian presence in Hollywood. Instead of reflecting God's grace, however, a sign at the entrance said, No Actors or Dogs Allowed.

Instead of loving and praying for actors, directors, and movie moguls, church people were boycotting and throwing out their televisions.

And to the Church, as far as they were concerned, to be a Christian in Hollywood meant you were either betraying the Church or betraying the industry.

If Karen had chosen to shine her light in Africa, the Church would have loved and supported her. Because she was trying to shine the light of Christ in Hollywood, she'd been cast as Judas in the war between light and darkness.

Dropping her head into her hands, she felt her throat choke with unshed tears. Karen was so *tired*. She was exhausted, not from the fine line she had to walk being an outspoken Christian in Hollywood, but from feeling betrayed by the very people who should have been praying for her.

She thought about people she knew: all the broken Christians who'd come to Hollywood and needed support and prayer. . .and the nonbelievers, scores and scores of them, who had no access to the Gospel.

"God, I want to see revival in Hollywood. I want to

see believers praying for nonbelievers," she prayed. "I want the Christians in Hollywood prayed for so they have support and are valued in this difficult, secular place to live and work. I want the church praying for the entertainment industry instead of hating! Please, God, what do you want me to do?" Karen prayed.

No sooner had her dangerous prayer ended than a thought began to crystallize in her mind. It was a truth that she and her husband, Jim, had discovered a few years before: that if you pray for someone, you can't hate them.

That's it! A lightbulb turned on in her mind. *If I could start a prayer network, we could get the Church to take all of that negative energy and PRAY instead of boycotting, hating, and writing angry letters.*

That was the birth of the Hollywood Prayer Network. Karen prayed the dangerous prayer in 1999 and launched the ministry in 2001.

As a producer, she knew starting a prayer network could lead to her losing her credibility. And if she was a vocal Christian, she might not get any more jobs. When she and Jim arrived in Hollywood in the early eighties, they had a hard time even finding other believers. People really thought if you told somebody you were a Christian, you'd lose your job. So most believers hid their faith or stayed under the radar.

And when she and Jim first came into the industry after college, it was a lot harder than they thought it was going to be living in the secular culture of Hollywood. . .especially with so little encouragement and only a few relationships with other believers. They wanted to stay strong in their faith but work in Hollywood, and it was challenging. They *needed* to find more Christians.

Somehow, they found six others and together started a prayer group that met in their home each month to pray for each other and other friends in the industry. It came to be known as Premise. They had been meeting for prayer together for ten years when Karen's idea of a network of prayer for Hollywood began to develop.

Her heart beat with excitement. But her logical mind gave her pause.

A national Hollywood Prayer Network? That would make Karen a very visible Christian. A target of criticism. Besides, she was a professional. How was founding a nonprofit to get people all over the country praying for Hollywood going to affect her career? She knew it was a big risk. And would she have enough time?

The more she thought about it, she knew. *I've got to do this. I've got to take a chance.*

She became more and more passionate about doing *whatever* God wanted her to in order to bridge the gap between the "Church" and Hollywood through prayer. She knew that people were dying spiritually and emotionally, that the divorce and drug-use rates were horrible. There were widespread affairs and rampant infidelity, as well as the domestic violence problem.

She'd heard people say that actors and stars didn't need prayer. They had fabulous houses and cars, fame and everything material they'd ever want. But Karen knew that even though some actors were celebrities with glamorous lives, underneath they were all real, struggling people with great needs. In fact, most of the actors in the Screen Actors Guild weren't able to support themselves. Only a small percentage of them could actually make a good living on their films and TV series. And though Hollywood had a glossy covering, Karen knew it was a place of broken lives and broken people who desperately needed prayer.

When she launched Hollywood Prayer Network in 2001, a lot of people in the Church didn't get it. Karen endured all kinds of criticism and received letters claiming it was a waste of time to pray for heathens. Some people thought she was starting the network for gain, to make money.

"No, I wouldn't pray for Hollywood; it's an evil place and I'm angry at the films and TV shows coming out of it," one person told her. That opinion was mirrored over and over by other believers.

The criticism made her more and more convinced she was doing the right thing. But how would she find the time? It would be a time-consuming ministry directing a national and later international network of intercessors. But she found she loved it. The ministry came into her and Jim's lives when their boys were young and she was working on a show that was so time-consuming that when she called home to talk to her boys, they were so angry they wouldn't even talk to their mom on the phone. So Karen cut back her work to part-time so she could spend more time with her boys and direct the Hollywood Prayer Network (HPN).

Jim's support meant the world during those beginning years of the ministry. The couple prayed together every day as they have continued to do throughout their thirty-one years of marriage—and they met monthly to pray for Hollywood in their group while leading other prayer events for HPN.

Yet as the network grew, she and Jim and their two boys went through a rough couple of years starting in 2005. Neither of them could find work or projects to be involved with. And even though Karen felt that she was doing what God had called her to do in founding and leading the Hollywood Prayer Network, they practically couldn't pay people to hire them. They were constantly stressed about not being able to pay their bills. They asked God whether they should sell their house, but they had no idea where they were going to go or what they'd do if things didn't turn around.

Throughout the hard times, Karen kept asking for their circumstances to change, and then it hit her. She needed to ask and seek for God to *change her*. Their financial and employment picture didn't get better immediately. Karen could have gotten discouraged and thrown in the towel on directing HPN. But they persevered and eventually things did turn around.

When Karen and Jim first came to Hollywood, they met only eight believers. Now there are over ten thousand, and those are just the ones they know of. At that time, parents refused to let their young people come to Hollywood to pursue a career. Now there are scores of talented young actors, writers, producers, and film school graduates working in the industry who are strong in faith and making an impact.

For twenty-three years, Karen and Jim's prayer

group and hundreds of other people have gathered and prayed on the evening of the National Day of Prayer. They and other intercessors take weekly prayer walks on studio lots in Hollywood. One week six people walk and pray around the Warner Brothers lot; the next week a different group will prayer walk around Paramount Studios; the following week around Universal Studios; and the next around Disney Studios. On the studio prayer walks, at their prayer meetings, and in the Premise prayer group, many prayers are lifted up:

"Lord, let Your will be done in my life and work here, and let me accept whatever You have for me."

"God, please supply my daily needs as I try to break in here in Hollywood. I need to pay my rent. Help me to trust You."

"Lord, please use me to be salt and light in this industry."

"Father, please open the hearts of my boss and co-workers so that they can embrace You and Your unconditional love. They need You so much and don't know it."

"Lord, may You bring in the right people to sell my project and bring me a strong production team to work with on this film."

"May the Christians have favor here to be in positions of influence and to be respected by the people around us."

"Lord, please grow our community of Christians so that we are strong and visible and loving. We want to change the Hollywood professionals' view of 'Christians' so they see that we are loving, nonjudgmental, supportive, peaceful, and excellent at our craft."

These are just a few of the millions of prayers being prayed by Christians *in Hollywood*.

Members of Karen and Jim's prayer group also take agency prayer walks, driving around agencies that represent the stars, writers, and directors. The agencies are made up of very powerful people who have great influence in the entertainment industry, and all need prayer. They also meet and do prayer walks all around the Dolby Theatre before the Academy Award shows.

And outside of Hollywood, millions of people are praying in the Hollywood Prayer Network, which has become a dynamic movement of prayer for the artists and professionals, projects and productions of the secular entertainment industry. This nonprofit ministry realizes the global impact of Hollywood, the world's most influential mission field, and seeks to cover it in prayer.

What has God been doing in the fourteen years since HPN was founded?

Fueled by thousands and thousands. . .even millions of prayers from countless HPN individuals and eighty-six prayer group chapters throughout the US and in twenty-nine countries, many in the church have begun to look at Hollywood as a mission field.

As they join their prayers, God has been doing miraculous things in the entertainment industry.

Karen and her coworkers send out a monthly e-mail with prayer requests so people know how to pray and know what the greatest needs are. And the ministry is not just for adults; young people also have joined in. Older kids can wear a red wristband featuring the numbers 90028—the world's most influential zip code.

Wearing it reminds them to pray for the entertainment industry and the people in it.

God is also changing the hearts of Christians *outside of Hollywood* through prayer, so that those inside don't receive so much anger in the form of boycotts and hate letters. Instead of hating, they are learning to support those in the entertainment mission field with their prayers. They pray for the decision-makers, the influencers, and the Christian and non-Christian actors and directors in the thirty-mile radius around Los Angeles.

"We're trying to build a community here who are artists, who love the Lord, who won't compromise," said Karen. They're seeing a visible difference in the number of people following Jesus within the industry who are unifying and praying.

Also, God is bringing more strong believers with a missions mind-set to work in the entertainment industry; they are having an impact. These people want to create good products and at the same time reach their friends and coworkers with the Gospel. Now Christians are not so afraid to let people know they follow Jesus. That's a big change.

In addition, Karen and Jim are seeing more non-believers seeking God, Jesus, spirituality, and life answers than ever before. More Jewish people are accepting Jesus as their Messiah and are very open to having conversations about God and Jesus. Another huge change!

With one courageous woman's dangerous prayer and her willingness to put feet to her prayer, a whole industry is being impacted. An industry that in many ways has more influence on American life than even the government, especially for the younger generations.

As Karen says, "The church is the theater today. Sunday school is the television, and hymns are Pandora and iTunes. That's where we are getting our influence."

She's not trying to get *everyone* to pray for Hollywood—just the people who really care about the influence that media and the entertainment industry have and those who want to see change. "I'm trying to reach the people who are already passionate about the media or movies, but their passion comes out in anger and disapproval," Karen explains. "Everyone needs prayer, so go to the places you're passionate about." She challenges people to channel their anger through prayer, which makes an eternal difference.

In the fourteen years since Karen prayed her dangerous prayer, the Hollywood Prayer Network[13] has mobilized millions of people to pray. God has done more than she could have asked or thought or imagined (Ephesians 3:20), and He has plans and purposes yet to be revealed in the media and entertainment industry not only in the United States but also around the world.

Chapter Nine

ON THE WINDS OF GOD'S PLAN

Great revivals always begin in the hearts of a few men and women whom God arouses by his Spirit to believe in him as a living God. They believe he is a God who answers prayer. Upon their heart he lays a burden from which no rest can be found except in persistent crying unto God.

R. A. TORREY

A group of fifteen people stood on the hill overlooking the town of Eugene, Oregon. Since it was the tallest point above the city, they had an almost 300-degree view of downtown and the green hills to the south. In the warm summer evening, the orangey balsam scent of fir trees filled the air. From their vantage point on the clearing, they could see over the tops of the trees, down to the Willamette River, the University of Oregon campus, and the foothills and forests to the south, east, and west of town.

On that summer night, however, as beautiful as the view was, the group wasn't there for sightseeing.

They were on the hill to pray for the city.

In 1991 Eugene was one of the least churched cities in the Pacific Northwest. It was filled with college students, old hippies leftover from the sixties, outdoorsy hikers and adventurers, long-distance bikers, runners, and retired artists and creative folks. Eugene also had a high population of homeless individuals and always attracted a fair number of runaway youth, some with mental health and addiction problems.

The predominant religion of the area in the early nineties was New Age, which accompanied the hippie culture and could be witnessed weekly at a downtown event called the Saturday Market, where a couple of city blocks were occupied by tie-dyed goods, food vendors, handcrafted items, and of course some open pot smoking. There were two large (five thousand plus) churches in town, but they represented a world that was not of interest to the countercultural folks who made up a large portion of the population. Both camps kept their distance from one another.

Dan Schmieding and his wife, Pam, were part of a small start-up church of about forty people who began praying a dangerous prayer: "Lord, bring spiritual renewal to our notoriously unchurched community."

From the beginning, the verse that inspired their prayer was 2 Chronicles 7:14 (NIV): "If my people, who are called by my name, will humble themselves and pray and seek my face and turn from their wicked ways, then I will hear from heaven, and I will forgive their sin and will heal their land."

They had a passion for prayer and for seeing their city turn to God. As their prayer efforts took shape, they met once a week on the top of the hill and prayed over the city.

Other evenings they walked through the streets in small groups, quietly praying over the neighborhoods.

"Lord, bring revival to the people in these homes. Renew their hearts. Draw them to You."

"Wake up those who are spiritually sleeping and apathetic."

"Bring a move by Your Spirit that would stir people's hearts and change lives."

They also prayed in Bible studies and discussed prayer and revival in more detail. During this time, they shared their vision of spiritual renewal with a couple of other small churches who were praying by themselves. Those people committed to joining them to pray once or twice a month in the effort to reach the city.

Together they prayed:

"Bring a whole revival touching everybody in Eugene. God, move in some way!"

"Soften people's hearts, including our own, and prepare us for what You want to do."

"Touch people's hearts! Return us to our first love."

Their prayers went in two related directions. In one direction, they prayed that the Spirit of God would move in some tangible ways that would draw people away from witchcraft, New Age ideology, and the drug/ alcohol culture.

In the second yet equally essential direction, they prayed for unity within the Christian churches because their initial meetings with a few church leaders indicated that there was very little cooperation between churches in the area. They all seemed to have "turf" to protect and were somewhat resistant to forming a unified effort for any purpose.

During this time, in the early 1990s, a couple of big stadium events happened in Eugene—one a Greg Laurie event, the other a Promise Keepers extravaganza (which did generate good intra-church cooperation). However, their little group was more interested in seeing a long-term, locally initiated and organized effort that would be specifically tailored for their unique area rather than an outside, prepackaged operation that would come and then be gone.

Along the way, while studying revivals in history, Dan realized that sometimes revivals followed turmoil or adversity in the areas where they took place.

This idea was bantered about in the group and even may have led to a reduction in the fervency of the praying activity in some of the members. It's one thing to pray for revival but quite another to think about what it might take to prompt people already in a strong comfort zone to turn in a new spiritual direction!

"We'd like to be able to say, 'Whatever it takes, Lord,'" Dan said. "But in reality, who wants to invite an unknown 'whatever' into their life?"

Nevertheless, the group continued praying. In the beginning the whole church prayed, and then they splintered off into a group of fifteen people who prayed more regularly—in their homes, on the hill overlooking the town, and through the streets.

After four or five months of doing this every week, the people wondered what was next. They saw nothing happening and got discouraged. They couldn't identify even a small bit of solid evidence that God was doing anything. Although the group of praying people eventually decreased in size as some dropped out, a small core continued.

In time, however, the prayer sessions stopped altogether.

But God never forgot their prayers. . . . As E. M. Bounds said, "God shapes the world by prayer. Prayers are deathless. They outlive the lives of those who uttered them."

Several months later, things started to pick up in a tangible way when doors opened to serve the homeless. A local rescue mission invited them to make presentations during their chapel services one night a month. Dan and his group did some dramas and individual testimonies where they shared the difference Jesus had made in their lives. They put a band together and led singing and worship at the mission. Initially they had only a band and one or two people who would share a message, but they continued to serve at the mission monthly.

Dan was invited to do a weekly Bible study at the local jail and outreach at the correctional work camp in the area. One thing led to another as the group was led along by the wind of God's plan.

At the same time, they decided to get to know the homeless population better and see what needs there were and how they could help. The group put together an outreach in a big city park for the homeless and other underserved members of the community. They provided a barbecue dinner and music, and many people showed up.

Volunteers struck up conversations with homeless individuals or working poor people who'd come for the food. The volunteers listened to their stories and then shared their own. When the band took a break, someone shared a testimony or a story of God working in their life.

Dan's church group continued to find opportunities to share God's love. And sometimes they partnered with other groups in the area to put on more barbecues.

At the informal park gatherings, when they asked other churches that had worship bands to show up and help, they joined in. Three or four of the local churches were willing to participate, but left to themselves, they couldn't come up with ideas. Since Dan and his group were already putting on the barbecue monthly and had all of the needed supplies, they continued to cosponsor the barbecue and bring their own volunteers until it snowballed and more people got involved.

They had expected God to show up and do something dramatic in answer to their prayers. But instead He was preparing *them* to serve and get involved in what He was doing within the poor in their community. The prayers were essential to get them ready to serve. Instead of the fast renewal they'd hoped for, it was a slow development. But as Dan looks back, he knows God was leading.

The barbecue and music in the park outreach grew until they were feeding two to three hundred people every month. Dan and his group put in their own money. They also got donations and volunteers from different churches to participate and made good contacts with local food banks.

When the weather got cold, they rented an indoor venue and held music concerts, where they provided food and clothes, coats and necessities to homeless people. They got sleeping bags from sporting goods stores and loads of socks. Volunteers did face painting for the children and gave haircuts.

They eventually became a semi-organized nonprofit organization called Free People, which has no paid staff and still works today providing small-scale service to about forty to sixty homeless participants per week.

Many volunteers have come and gone, and the

group of down-and-outers has steadily increased over time. But as Dan says, "I guess our prayers for renewed hearts has come about, albeit not in the miraculous biblical proportions everybody was hoping to see. And the renewed hearts are not only [those of] the homeless whom we targeted in ministry, but also ours. It turns out when people from other groups are invited to volunteer in ways they previously haven't, an interesting change comes over them, too."

Eight or nine years ago, the group rented a building that became a homeless church down by the river. Every week a core group of thirty people show up, eat, and then worship and hear a fifteen-minute message.

People who used to be homeless but were able to get on their feet get a chance to serve others. It turns people around and gives them hope to get out of the receiving end of things and be part of the volunteer group that sets up and serves food. They begin to feel that God is working in their lives, that He's brought them out of the helpless place to be the ones offering the help.

The best feedback Dan and his group get comes from the guy who says, "I consider this my church. I feel like I belong here," and then goes on to help set up tables, grill on the barbecue, or make potato salad. Whereas he used to think he had nothing to offer, now he's grateful for the opportunity to pitch in and serve others.

Dan and some involved in this project from the beginning have actually grown financially poorer in the course of the ministry. In his self-employed public relations and graphic designer job, he couldn't take on as much work. His wife taught school and God provided as he spent more time in ministry and sought to balance work, family, and outreach.

But Dan says, "When you're involved in a cause you feel God has led you to, it turns out that losing or not being able to acquire some materialistic things turns out to be less consequential and important than you first imagined."

As Dan has followed where God has led, he has been surprised by what happened: If you'd asked him twenty-five years ago if he'd be teaching a Bible study and counseling weekly at the jail, he would have said, "No, never." Yet that is exactly what he does along with leading the other outreach efforts. This is nothing he could have planned on his own. Long ago, he would have said, "There's no way I'm going to do that. I wouldn't know how to get started or the first thing about leading."

"It all goes back to the time we started praying. We want to pray for big things, not small things. If we pray for revival," Dan says, "we want the whole city. The reality is there are little opportunities God gives us to put feet to our prayers."

There are still a lot of homeless people in Eugene. The economy hasn't fully recovered yet. So Dan's church group is still doing the outreach to the homeless and working poor once a month.

On Sunday afternoons, when Dan joins the others at the church on the hill, he remembers those many prayers for revival they prayed on that same hill twenty-five years ago as they watched the river run by.

For the down-and-out people to get excited about getting together every Sunday and being on the serving side of the table—that's revival. To be able to bring the love of Christ to people in a practical way week after week—that's revival.

For churches to join together to do something bigger than they could do on their own—that's revival.

And those prayers? They were necessary for ground-breaking, preparing them to join God in practical ministry to homeless people. He softened hearts. He touched people with His love and continues to every Sunday when they meet for church and every time they have monthly barbecues and outreach in the park.

"Do not despise these small beginnings, for the LORD rejoices to see the work begin," says Zechariah 4:10 (NLT).

Through those small beginnings of prayer and the work God led them to do to serve the poor in their community, God *is* bringing renewal to Eugene one person at a time, and He will continue to do so, one person at a time, one prayer at a time.

Chapter Ten

THE BOX OF CHOCOLATES

Will God ever ask you to do something you are not able to do? The answer is yes—all the time! It must be that way, for God's glory and kingdom. If we function according to our ability alone, we get the glory; if we function according to the power of the Spirit within us, God gets the glory. He wants to reveal Himself to a watching world.

Henry Blackaby

Katherine knelt with her friend Kelli on the cream-colored carpet in Kelli's living room one afternoon in the fall of 2013. The two women met often to pray. They were so in love with the Lord, they'd rather spend time with Him in prayer rather than chatting with other moms at the local coffee shop or going shopping.

But several months into their prayer journey, a shift happened.

From requesting things for their families and children, even for themselves, they realized there was a difference between praying out of their thoughts and emotions and praying what was on God's heart. A difference between praying *their agenda* and praying *God's agenda.*

"Lord, show me what's on Your heart!" Katherine prayed. That was the cry of her spirit. As the clouds outside lifted and light filtered into the room, she felt her heart floating on hope and expectation.

Katherine and Kelli were both active in a new ministry called Watershed. They met first in homes and then later at a church next to a nearby university campus where they learned how to listen to God and be led by the Holy Spirit. They had learned, as Psalm 62 describes, to wait in silence, giving God time and opportunity to convey His thoughts. On this particular day the two women spent time worshipping and waiting, asking what the Lord wanted them to pray about.

"What is on Your heart, God?"

In the quiet moments that followed, into Katherine's imagination appeared a picture of many international students, both males and females. Different colors of young people from different nations were seated in chairs at the Watershed training center, singing and learning about the Holy Spirit. As the image unfolded, she described it to Kelli and they both began to ask the Lord, "How can this be?"

At that time she didn't know even one student from another country or have any idea how this would take place. Although there were many international students on the University of Central Oklahoma campus, she didn't have any connections with the campus ministries that had outreaches to them or with the English Language Institute where they often took classes.

It could have ended there if she had depended on what she'd done in the past or was familiar with. The whole idea seemed to be out of her wheelhouse. How would she be able to do this? She had no idea.

Katherine and Kelli prayed, asking God to accomplish what He'd shown her. They prayed that the nations would come to know Christ. That the doors would be open to minister to those who were ripe for the truth and ready for His love and grace in their lives. They asked Him to

- open the door so they could get to know some international students,
- open the door for them to know men as well as women, and
- bring opportunities to share about the Holy Spirit with these young people.

While they were praying, Katherine sensed that God had authored this prayer, although she was clueless about how any of it was going to unfold.

An hour after she left Kelli's house, she was pushing her cart through a big department store when her cell phone rang. Her friend Tiffany was on the other end of the line and said, "Katherine, I was praying just now and God gave me a picture of you with a box of chocolates. You were picking the chocolates up one at a time, tasting each one. Each of the chocolates was delicious and unique, and you were thoroughly enjoying every bite. I saw you with all these chocolates—like gifts. Then the verse came to mind, 'Taste and see that the Lord is good,' and you started sharing these chocolates with other people."

Standing in an aisle at Nordstrom's listening to her friend, Katherine felt like her heart was about to burst. She sensed that each one of the chocolates represented different shades of brown, representing international students she was going to meet and with whom she would share God's gifts and goodness.

From that point on, she made phone calls and discussed strategies with her ministry teammates. She asked, "How can we get the students to Watershed? Can we have an evening gathering since they have classes and work all day?" She pitched out ideas.

Since Katherine was an artist, she decided to offer free art classes to international students. She made up flyers and distributed them on campus. The halls of the university echoed with excitement as students rushed from class to class, talking and texting. Caught up in the rush, Katherine made her way to the bulletin boards to post flyers about the free art classes. Back home, she waited with anticipation for the phone to ring.

The silence was deafening. No one, it seemed, was interested in her art classes.

Wait, what? Lord, I thought You wanted me to minister to international students! How is this going to happen?

The more she talked about her ideas and tried to figure out ways to accomplish them, the more frustrated she became. She had exhausted her own efforts and didn't know what to do. As the weeks went on, one door after another closed.

Not sure what else to do, she sat in silence, surprised when the Lord dropped a message in her heart: "You don't have to do anything or figure this out. I will bring the students to your doorstep."

Finally she stopped striving and trusted God was well able to accomplish His purposes. Rolling the care of it onto the Lord, she left for a trip to Israel.

But when she returned in December, she couldn't shake the vision about international students.

So she knocked on a few doors again to see if a path would open up. She talked to more people about her desire to reach out to international students.

A few weeks later, when she was visiting with her neighbor Cyndi, she told her she felt God's call to work with international students.

"Heidi, one of my friend's daughters, is a junior and works in the international student office on campus,"

Cyndi replied. "She's recruiting host families for international students. Not only that, she's looking for volunteers right now to host these young people. I have an e-mail from her I'll forward to you."

Katherine's excitement grew like that of a child waiting to see what's inside the packages under the Christmas tree as she typed an e-mail to Heidi. She told her all about Watershed and asked if any international students might want to come to this ministry. They agreed to visit on the phone before Christmas.

When they talked, Katherine discovered Heidi was head of CRISP, the Citizens Responding to International Students Program. She learned more about what Heidi was looking for: local families to accept international students as their surrogate families until the students left to go back to their country. To invite them for holidays, include them in family occasions, and have them over for a meal once a month.

In the midst of Heidi's presentation of CRISP's goals, Katherine told her about the vision God had given her and how He'd spoken to her. "Do you think our ministry can be of benefit to international students? I'd love to meet you face-to-face. I want to help these young people." They agreed to meet for lunch a few days later.

Heidi was clearly intrigued that Katherine would talk very naturally about the Holy Spirit and about having a vision. She'd never heard anybody talk about those kinds of things.

Their lunch led to weekly meetings where they got to

know each other and share ideas. Ultimately their time together developed into a very dear friendship.

What Katherine had *thought* was going to be a relationship with international students started with one college student—not an international student but an American. They had phone and text conversations and Katherine became a kind of mother figure to Heidi.

In the next few months, the two women read books together and did life together. Katherine prayed with and for Heidi. She had her over for dinner and her daughters loved her; it became a sweet and special relationship with the whole family.

Then in May, when Heidi had just turned twenty-one, she was diagnosed with thyroid cancer. The morning of Heidi's surgery, she asked Katherine to pick up her Armenian friend from Cyprus named Ani and bring her along to the hospital.

On the drive to Norman Regional, Ani asked Katherine, "I want to know about your faith. Heidi told me about it."

As Katherine shared about her journey with the Holy Spirit, Ani soaked up what she said like a sponge. The two connected and became friends. Ani's faith was intact, but she was hungry for more. From that day on, she became part of Katherine's family, joining them for meals, holidays, and Sundays. She had a vibrant prayer life and faith and wanted to go to Watershed with Katherine.

Over the summer, Heidi embraced Katherine and her husband like parents. Several times she asked them to pick up international students flying into the Oklahoma City airport.

On one of these occasions, Katherine and her husband went to the airport at midnight to welcome a group of seven students from India. Wide-eyed and excited about their first time on American soil, the students piled into their SUV. As they drove through the city and out to the university campus, they couldn't believe there weren't a million people on the streets.

One of the guys had a dream on the trip over, and when he told Katherine about it, she interpreted it. She connected almost instantly with the group of students. Although still holding on to his Hindi religion, Sachin, one of the Indian students they were transporting to the university, told her he was open to God and the Holy Spirit.

On the Fourth of July, Ani and Heidi spent the evening with Katherine's family, eating and watching fireworks. Heidi brought souvenirs from India where she'd spent the month of June. In mid-July she asked for help with other students. And thankfully, Katherine and her husband became official CRISP host family volunteers.

Later that summer, Heidi recruited them to help with nine Iraqi students, all men in their late twenties and thirties, who came to the university for ten weeks to study on a Fulbright scholarship. Katherine and her husband served as the CRISP family for three of them, and her friends Tiffany and Justin and a few other local families took the other Iraqi students. Some of the men were professors; several were in research and other fields. The families took them sightseeing and hosted them at their homes.

Two of the Iraqis were very religious Shiites, another a Sunni man from Baghdad, and several were Kurds, so initially a palpable tension crackled between them. Yet as the men came to the families' homes for dinners and cooked for them, played games, showed them their dances, and ate together, by the end of the ten weeks a unity had emerged among the men even though they were from different sects of Islam. They all entered into conversations about their faith and were very open to discuss differences.

In late August when the students from Iraq left to go back to their country, new students came to their door: Nakki and her boyfriend, Lance, from China, Carla from Brazil, and later her friend Alerson, and Esther from Germany.

Ani continued to be like a daughter, and Katherine's relationship with Heidi grew. She was glad God had given her family resources to be generous, to entertain, and to love and support so many international students. Through Facebook and other social media outlets, they kept up relationships with the students who'd returned home.

Katherine had seen a vision of students from other countries coming in the doors of a Watershed event, but it didn't happen that way.

They came through the door of her own home.

She asked God what was on His heart and He

answered: *international students!* He wanted her to join Him in showing His love to these people from around the world.

So many doors opened, but it didn't look at all like Katherine thought. While she initially believed students from other countries would be streaming through the doors of the Watershed training center, what God had in mind was something very personal and relational. Watershed gave her the ability to meet people as they were, with no fear or agenda, and feeling no responsibility for them to sign the Jesus card, but just to enjoy getting to know and love them.

As she sat at her dinner table at Thanksgiving last year, surrounded by her husband, her nineteen-, seventeen-, fourteen-, and thirteen-year-old daughters, and international students from several different countries, Katherine remembered a conference she'd attended nine months before her vision.

During one of the sessions, she experienced a moment of total clarity in which God spoke to her on the inside saying, "You're a mom; I've called you to be a mother of many." He reminded her of hopes and dreams that hadn't come to fruition in the past: disappointment over not being able to get into the foster program and hearing of a child who needed a family but not being chosen to be her mother.

Soon after the conference, she and her four girls and their friends were in the parking lot of their church while the girls were piling out of the car. A man came by and said, "There she is, the mother of many!"—an encouraging confirmation from someone who didn't even know her.

First came the Armenian student from Cyprus, then the Indian students. Next came the Iraqi students, then the Brazilian, Chinese, and German students. So far, Katherine and her family have reached out to more than twelve international students, in addition to those students' friends and students in other countries. She has hosted them in their home and thoroughly enjoyed becoming friends with them.

It wasn't exactly the path she'd planned, but when we are willing to pray dangerous prayers and follow God's guidance, He leads us on as great a journey as Katherine's.

And Heidi? Over time, she admitted that shortly before she and Katherine met, she'd had a crisis of faith and announced to her parents that she'd renounced God and Christianity. She'd tried Buddhism and had planned to travel to India to pursue Hinduism. She felt there was something more and was striving to discover what it was, searching to find her own faith. Her parents were worried and didn't know how to communicate with her or handle her spiritual struggles.

A year later, Heidi's spiritual journey is still in progress, and she remains close to Katherine and their family. At this point she knows there's a God and feels His love and grace in her life.

Students from different parts of the world continue to come to Katherine's front door and join her family around the table. Who knows what's ahead for Katherine or for Heidi, Ani, and the many international students

Katherine continues to invite into her home as she continues building relationships and is abandoned to God?

As Oswald Chambers wrote in *My Utmost for His Highest*, "When we are abandoned to God, He works through us all the time."[14]

Chapter Eleven

A PLEA FOR GOD'S HELP

Hope is the thing with feathers
That perches in the soul
And sings the tune without the words
And never stops at all.
EMILY DICKINSON

Ashley's arms and legs trembled uncontrollably. Her thinking became more torturous, reaching into her mind to pull out all the bad memories and pain. *I've failed. I'm a burden. I've disappointed my family. I'm going crazy, and there's no hope.* Her stomach churned with nausea, and she was so dizzy she couldn't even think of getting up.

Her body shook all throughout the night with the effects of pills and booze and sadness over what she'd become. She had despaired of life and considered ending the awful struggle that her existence had become, but something kept her sitting on that bed during those hours.

All she could utter was, "Help. Please."

Ashley's plea for God's help—in whatever form possible—came at a moment when she didn't even know if her Creator cared, when she thought that help might be an impossibility. She was risking everything, for if He was silent, she didn't know how she could go on.

Her internal world had been invaded by ill-fated biochemistry: within a few years, severe postpartum depression turned to chronic depression and eventually a desperation so consuming, so dark and relentless, that it filled her with a desire to end it all. It felt as if the heartache would never go away. The world seemed cold and mean with silence and didn't care to wrap its arms around her. It only enveloped her with its darkness.

This emotional descent was mirrored by her external world crumbling around her due in part to a progressive addiction to pain pills. What had started as trying to self-medicate just to appear more normal to her family and friends turned into something that was destroying her. Drinking made her more conversational but also brought a bigger nightmare.

At the moment she made her plea, Ashley thought herself beyond help, beyond the love of her Creator, beyond any hope of being the mother, daughter, wife, and friend she thought she was supposed to be. It seemed as if she were on a precipice, holding on to a thin ledge of shale, losing her grip on everything at once and about to career down the steep cliff.

In that moment, she didn't see how God could or would even want to help her. Losing a sense of hope and mental clarity, she saw everything as looking dark, and she felt—even when around her family—totally alone.

That night Ashley's plea was unconsciously accompanied by the expectation that rejection likely would follow. And rejection from God would bring excruciating pain to her already aching heart. As David expressed four thousand years ago, "Long enough, GOD— you've ignored me long enough. I've looked at the back of your head long enough. Long enough I've carried this ton of trouble, lived with a stomach full of pain" (Psalm 13:1 MSG). If the skies were brass and no help came from heaven, she had no idea what she'd do.

With her brain impaired by out-of-whack neurochemistry, Ashley had thought her only out was to leave her home and family and let her addiction take her as far as they would or end her life completely.

The morning came. Her body still shook and the

nausea was unbearable. Yet Ashley grabbed for her phone, almost without knowing what she was doing, and called a friend. This was the first of a series of unexpected "answers" to her simple, desperate prayer, "Help. Please."

Something inside her wanted to live, was fighting to live, even more than she wanted to maintain her image, her reputation, her banal attempts to achieve perfection.

Her friend came immediately over to her house and sat with her, holding her shaking body. Without words or judgment or shock, she listened while the dam broke and Ashley came clean with everything she'd been holding in, hiding, and self-medicating to deny.

Help came in the form of the unconditional acceptance of a friend's presence—in the form of complete and total honesty. No more hiding. With this new transparency, the first cell of relief was released into her bloodstream, and hope seemed like a minute but real possibility.

As her friend sat and spoke a few words of comfort, Ashley's brain fog still overwhelmed most of her senses. Her friend made a few calls, one to a family member to explain the dire need for help that Ashley couldn't herself explain or ask for yet. Another call was to a treatment facility. She asked Ashley if she'd be willing to consider going.

Up to this point Ashley would have thought treatment or rehab an impossibility for "someone like her." She'd never need to go to a place like that. So her answer was accompanied by tears and brought a few more cells of relief to her bloodstream. A fragile hope began to emerge.

"Yes. Please. I cannot do this on my own anymore."

Help came in the form of a strange, sterile, hospital-like building and the people who inhabited it with her for ninety days.

When she arrived, she set her small suitcase down and looked around at the nurses' station and the nondescript rooms with tan walls. An old TV sat in the center of the big room, and a few people in the corner drank coffee and played Scrabble on an old card table. Tears formed in the corners of her eyes while she watched the assistant director rifle through her bag to make sure she hadn't brought any forbidden items. Her thoughts began to race with negative what-ifs, but something—or Someone—told her this was the right place for her to be.

What would her friends think? As it turned out, she did lose many old friends in the process of "getting clean," but once she was on the other side of treatment, this loss didn't seem so important. Her reputation no longer mattered like it did for so long.

What mattered was finding hope. What mattered was realizing the prayer she prayed with barely a mustard seed of faith landed in the hands of God. What mattered was taking the most courageous step of faith she'd taken up to that point.

This was the great paradox that guided her back into the land of the living, back to her Creator, her family. When you're weak, He is strong. He uses the foolish things to shame the wise.

Ashley had let go of the need and drive and

delusion to fix herself and those around her when she finally uttered a wholehearted "Help." The uncertainty and danger of not knowing what the answer would be or whether God would care at all had been real. The fear of where that cry for help would lead her was there, but she didn't care because she was out of options and answers. She was sick and tired of being sick and tired. She couldn't fake good or happy or healthy anymore.

God responded to her simple plea. He helped her. Through the most unexpected place and people: a treatment facility with fellow addicts and alcoholics who shared their experiences. In a place she never would have imagined being, she discovered it was just the kind of place where the God she grew up hearing Bible stories about hangs out: a place where those who are desperate seek help, a place where God's grace creates hope and positive expectations, a place inhabited by people—even her—whom He loves unconditionally.

Ashley met Jesus in the understanding eyes of the chaplain, who accepted her and assured her of God's love when she was struggling with guilt-laden thoughts, and in the wisdom of her counselor who helped her see things she'd never realized about herself and her addictions. She heard Jesus giving her and others strength and hope in the nightly meetings as the residents shared around the circle. And He met her every morning when the sun came shining through her tiny room, giving her hope and help for another day.

That is the mystery that keeps bringing her to her knees every morning and every night, despite what happens in the in-between time in the midst of her fluctuating brain chemistry or cravings or blessings or mistakes. She still utters the prayer, "Help. Please." And she learned the addendum prayer that has become an anthem of her life: "Thank You. So much. Thank You."

Chapter Twelve

HANNAH'S PRAYER OF RELEASE

When the love of a mother for her child is connected with God's power through prayer, an irresistible force is released that changes people and situations and can even impact a nation and world.
CHERI FULLER

Ask most mothers and they'll tell you the hardest part of motherhood isn't giving birth—even if it is a long and difficult labor. Breastfeeding is arduous and full of challenges for some new moms. So is finding ways to get your baby to sleep if she prefers to be up all night wanting to eat and play. Dealing with toddler tantrums and occasional mommy guilt and sleep deprivation is challenging. But those aren't the very hardest things about motherhood.

Surveys, the experiences of hundreds of mothers from around the world, and my extensive interviews show that *letting go* is actually the hardest work of mothering. *Letting go* when your cute little boy or girl gets on the big yellow bus for the first time to go to kindergarten, lunch box in hand. *Letting go* when you wave good-bye as she goes to her first week of camp.

Letting go when your daughter asks for the keys because she just got her driver's license and wants to go it alone that day. *Letting go* when a boy with a corsage shows up at your door and your pretty girl goes on her first date to the school's winter ball. *Letting go* when she piles her clothes, shoes, laptop, iPad, and miscellaneous boxes of towels and linens into her car and leaves for college or for an apartment out of state for a job. That's a tough one!

One of the last but most final releases a mother needs to make is *letting go* when your child walks down the aisle to the arms of her waiting groom, gets married, and leaves home for good.

Just think: Hannah in the Bible never got to go

through any of those stages, not even the waving good-bye as her firstborn went into his first school classroom or away to camp for a week.

She had to release her son far earlier and in a much more final way, for he would never live with her again.

Hannah had struggled with infertility for years, even while her husband's other wife (can you imagine it—having to deal with the *other wife* and live with her in the same house?) had already been blessed with several children.

Hannah wanted a child more than anything but had been unable to conceive. Not only had Peninnah, her husband's other wife, had several children with Elkanah, but she also regularly taunted Hannah for her barrenness, driving her pain even deeper.

Elkanah loved his wife Hannah dearly, but he couldn't really understand her agony. "Hannah, why do you weep and why do you not eat and why is your heart sad?" he asked her. "Am I not better to you than ten sons?"

Apparently not. Hannah was sure she wanted a child of her own.

Year after year the whole family went up from their town to worship and sacrifice to the Lord at Shiloh. Elkanah always gave a double portion of meat to Hannah because he loved her so much and because the Lord had "closed her womb."

Year after year Peninnah ruined the trip to the temple because she taunted, maligned, and provoked Hannah until she wept and lost her appetite even while the others were eating the sacrificial meal.

The story could have ended here. But Hannah was a persevering woman who didn't give up. That's one of the things I love about our Hannah—her persistence and determination, along with the fact that she never gave up on God.

And most of all, her courage to pray a dangerous prayer.

On this particular trip, she poured out her request to the Lord. While thousands of women prayed before Hannah lived, hers is the "first recorded instance of a woman at prayer."[15]

Not only was Hannah's prayer one of the most difficult and dangerous prayers a mother could pray—the ultimate letting go of her child—it was also important enough to be the *first recorded prayer in the Bible by a woman*.

Through tears and bitter weeping, Hannah prayed and made a vow to God: "O Lord of Heaven's Armies, if you will look upon my sorrow and answer my prayer and give me a son, then I will give him back to you. He will be yours for his entire lifetime, and as a sign that he has been dedicated to the Lord, his hair will never be cut" (1 Samuel 1:11 NLT).

Her groans were so deep, the Bible says, that while her lips moved, no words came out. Seeing her, the priest Eli accused her of being drunk. Hannah's answer to Eli was straight on: "No, my lord, I am a woman of sorrowful spirit. I have drunk neither wine nor intoxicating drink, but have poured out my soul before the Lord" (1 Samuel 1:15 NKJV).

Eli then gave her his blessing and asked God to grant her request. Hannah left the temple, no longer burdened and sad, but knowing that her prayer had been heard and received by the Lord. The next morning she rose up and worshipped God.

Scripture tells us that the Lord did hear her prayer and granted her great desire to bear a child. In time Samuel was born to Elkanah and Hannah. What a day of rejoicing that must have been. How absolute bliss must have filled Hannah's heart.

A mother at last.

I have a feeling that Hannah didn't put little Samuel in daycare or even the temple nursery when they went to the annual sacrifice in Shiloh. No, she nurtured little Samuel day after day. She delighted in her little boy and gave him all the love and care a mother could give.

Then when he was weaned, the time came for her to fulfill her vow and take Samuel to the temple to live and serve God. Think of this: he was probably no more than three years old. And this was not preschool, a sleepover, or college she was releasing her little boy to—it was forever. Never again would she hold him in her arms when he was sad or ill. Never again would she get to feed him breakfast, have him sleep under her roof, or see him run in the village with the other children.

For after that day of release, she would see her beloved firstborn son only once a year. How difficult it must have been for her to let go of him, the child she prayed and wept for!

But she had trusted God to answer her prayer, this

dangerous prayer, and had made a vow to the Lord. However, she wasn't putting her little one into the hands of trusted, responsible, and loving adults. No, she was putting him into the care of Eli, a washed-up reprobate of a priest and a very poor, permissive father to his two corrupt sons.

Nonetheless, she trusted her boy to God's safekeeping. In doing so, she dedicated him to the Lord's service in the temple for the rest of his life.

I think that letting go must have been very difficult in itself, but just think about sending your little boy of only three years old into a corrupt environment. Even though it was the Lord's temple Hannah was taking her boy to, it wasn't a godly environment. Eli's sons were evil and worthless—very poor role models for Samuel—and the Bible tells us they didn't even know God. Eli's leadership was weak, and sin abounded in the temple. How could this old man be expected to raise and train her son?

Yet Hannah, a woman of great faith, kept her promise. Every year she stitched little Samuel a robe and took it to him at the temple. I can just picture her hemming the robe with love, every stitch a prayer—for God's protection and favor to surround her boy, for him to grow strong and wise, for God's glory and purpose to be accomplished in and through Samuel's life.

Did she gripe and argue with God, asking Him to make an exception and not make Samuel stay at the temple? No, she praised Him with all her heart even as she "lent" him to the Lord: "As long as he lives he shall be lent to the LORD" (1 Samuel 1:28 NKJV).

As she dedicated Samuel, she sang a song of praise that has endured throughout the ages:

> *"My heart rejoices in the LORD;*
> *in the LORD my horn is lifted high.*
> *My mouth boasts over my enemies,*
> *for I delight in your deliverance.*
> *There is no one holy like the LORD;*
> *there is no one besides you;*
> *there is no Rock like our God."*
>
> 1 SAMUEL 2:1–2 NIV

What was the first outcome of Hannah's bringing her need to God in prayer and trusting her child to Him? Her sorrow was turned to joy, her blessings multiplied. Later she had three more sons and two daughters. And her beloved firstborn son, Samuel, grew and became God's spokesperson at a time in history when words and visions from the Lord were rare.

As much as Hannah must have missed him, she had the joy of knowing that "the LORD was with Samuel as he grew up, and he let none of Samuel's words fall to the ground" (1 Samuel 3:19 NIV). Since God had some serious, heart-searching things to say to Eli and Israel, he spoke to them through the lips of a child.[16] Samuel had to learn to discern the voice of God in the temple at an early age and was called to service among the Israelites. Samuel became one of the greatest leaders of God's people in that time, the last of the judges before the king era, and the one who anointed David as king over Israel.

Although we may not have to relinquish our children to God at age three like Hannah did, we will be called upon to entrust our children to God's care at some point in their lives. We will be prompted to pray what seem like dangerous prayers. We can't put them in a protective bubble throughout childhood and adolescence. We can't control all the forces that threaten to undermine and undo our careful training and nurturing love. But we can follow Hannah's example by scooping our children up and carrying them to Jesus, who loves them far more than we ever could and will take the finest care of them while accomplishing His purpose in their lives.

Chapter Thirteen

SHACKLED BY SIN

Where the Spirit of the Lord is, there is freedom.
2 CORINTHIANS 3:17 NIV

One Sunday morning Jake sat in the sanctuary with his parents and a friend half-listening to the sermon. His thoughts were on a verse from Psalm 121: "I lift up my eyes to the mountains—where does my help come from? My help comes from the LORD, the Maker of heaven and earth" (vv. 1–2 NIV).

He wanted to believe that God could help and rescue him, but there he was sitting in church yet living a double life. For five years he'd been struggling with a serious addiction to pornography—a battle he was losing. He'd become a believer two years before, but his addiction took even his love of God hostage. It's not that he didn't pray. He did—usually while looking at disgusting pornography sites on the Internet. Lust consumed him, and the worst part was that he felt utterly powerless to change.

When he first saw the porn sites while at a sleep-over with several friends, he wanted to be "cool," even though he was a little shocked at first. Out of curiosity, he kept his eyes on the screen as the boys scrolled through image after image on porn websites. Then he thought they were exciting. When he looked for the sites at home, he got more and more interested in what he saw.

Whenever he could use the computer—when his parents were asleep or out for the evening, when they weren't looking or out in the yard—he'd spend time looking at graphic, degrading images. While in the beginning some of the photos disgusted him, they also aroused him and got his hormones going. Yet he hated being tormented at night by horrible dreams and by day by debilitating guilt. *I'm bad, and I know it. My parents would freak out. I've got to stop doing this.*

Nevertheless, pornography was like a drug he couldn't live without. He'd tell himself after a night full of seeking thrills and trash on the Internet that it wasn't too bad. The next morning he'd be disgusted by what he'd done and tell himself he wasn't ever going to look at it again, but by evening he'd lost his resolve and was back at the screen, mesmerized. So many times he'd prayed to be free, but God didn't seem to be listening.

As he sat in the pew that Sunday, he thought, *People at church think I'm a strong teen role model. Little kids look up to me because I'm an athlete and youth group leader. My parents think I'm a devoted Christian and tell me how proud they are of me. The truth is that I'm neither. I'm disgusting. I lift up my eyes to the hills, but help comes from nowhere for me.*

Seconds later, his attention was riveted to the words spoken from the pulpit: "The LORD detests those whose hearts are perverse, but he delights in those whose ways are blameless" (Proverbs 11:20 NIV).

God detests me? The thought shocked and horrified him. But why wouldn't He? Jake knew he was a hypocrite and a liar, but he had no earthly idea what to do about it. He was a failure in his faith. Even though he looked good on the outside and people thought highly of him, his ways were far from blameless. For the first time, he saw his addiction to pornography the way God saw it.

It broke his heart and crushed his spirit.

Bowing his head, he sent an urgent prayer to heaven. *God, if You are listening to me, hear my plea. I'm a sinner and a slave to my sin. I can't resist pornography even though I know it's wrong. God, save me! Whatever You need to do, do it! However You want to! I believe that You can, yet I'm still shackled. Relieve me of this burden—please! I have no other options.*

He hurried out of the church when the last song was sung, avoiding everyone he knew from his youth group. He ran home instead of riding with his parents. He didn't want to be with anybody. He didn't want to talk to anybody. At home, he fell on his bed and stared into space for half an hour until his mom knocked on the door.

"Jake," she said, stepping in. "I just got a call from your youth director. One of the other guys can't go to camp and the camp fee is nonrefundable. He wants to know if you'll go in his place. Interested?"

At first he thought it sounded boring. None of his best friends were going.

Then the thought occurred to him: *I need to get away from my computer and think about something else. Maybe it'll help me unplug for a week.*

"Yeah, I'll go. . . ."

"Are you all right? You don't sound very excited."

"Yeah, I'm okay, but would you leave, please, Mom? I need some time alone." His mom left his room, and he was left with his own dark thoughts.

God, I'm in a black pit and can't see light in any direction.

How do I break these bonds? How do I break this addiction? I pray and pray, but You don't seem to hear my cry for help. The Israelites waited four hundred years before You released them from bondage in Egypt. How long do I have to wait? Why won't You answer me?

A few hours later Jake left his room and discovered he had the house to himself. Immediately his mouth went dry as he looked at the computer sitting there, luring him.

He walked outside and paced around. He thought about taking a bike ride but was drawn back inside to the computer. It was so easy to hide it. When no one knew or watched what he was doing, he could go online and get access to hundreds of sexual pictures and videos. Just like a drug, it always caused him to want it more and more and spend more of his time on it. He had to look again.

Nobody will see.

He booted up and connected to the Internet. A Christian home page came up and he stared at it for a few minutes. Then, hating himself for doing it, he logged on to some porn sites.

He swallowed hard as lewd photos filled the screen. He was riveted to the images even as his heart beat faster and his excitement grew.

A few minutes later, he switched back to the Christian website, thinking his parents might be home soon.

Five words stared at him:

Jesus watches where you surf.

A pair of eyes followed his cursor as he moved it

across the screen. The words. . .the eyes. . .it was all too much. He fell across the keyboard, sobbing. "I'm a Christian who's hooked on looking at porn sites! God, forgive me and change me! Work something awesome in my life!"

The words on that screen still burned in his mind as he walked up the hill at youth camp a few days later. He saw three girls playing Ping-Pong and introduced himself to them. As they talked, he noticed that a light seemed to radiate from them. An unmistakable light. Their smiles, their attitudes, their words—it was the glow of Jesus in them.

It had been so long since he'd felt God's presence. His soul was as dry as the red dirt on the campground. But at that moment, being with those girls who seemed full of Christ, a warmth and love filled and satisfied him more than any lewd images ever had.

With sudden clarity he understood that pornography had controlled him because he'd tried to use it to fill a void for real love—the kind of void only Jesus could fill. He realized that pornography was like an evil plague that was killing his soul day by day.

He found a spot alone under a tree and rededicated his life to Jesus. Once again, he asked God to forgive his sin and give him the strength to resist. It was like time stood still and he was in the presence of Jesus, being washed of all the filth he'd immersed himself in.

When he got home from camp that weekend, the first thing he saw when he walked in the house was the computer. Cold fear gripped him. His mouth went dry.

His hands felt clammy.

It was time to confront the monster in his life. He longed to be free. Romans 6:17 (NLT) suddenly came to his mind: "Thank God! Once you were slaves of sin, but now you wholeheartedly obey this teaching we have given you."

Jake prayed, then turned and walked away from the computer.

That wasn't the only time he had to resist the temptation. In the months that followed, every time he turned on the computer for schoolwork or e-mails, he had to make the conscious decision to resist the pull of pornography. Months passed, but finally with God's help and many prayers, the day came when it wasn't a struggle anymore. He began to experience a sense of freedom and joy he hadn't known in a long time.

God not only delivered him from his addiction but also gave him the tools and the desire to help other guys break free from the shackles of pornography and other kinds of addiction.

Chapter Fourteen

LAUNCHING INTO THE DEEP

I know not by what methods rare,
But this I know: God answers prayer.
I know not if the blessing sought
Will come in just the guise I thought,
I leave my prayer to Him alone
Whose will is wiser than my own.
ELIZA HICKOK

It happened in a brick country church in Franklin Springs, Georgia, on New Year's Day many years ago. Along with many families in the community, Barbara and her husband, Bane, and their two young children walked down the center aisle. They strolled between two rows of oak-stained pews, stopping to greet friends and extended family members.

As the light shone through the big stained glass windows, memories flooded in: of the day when Barbara, a young college student, met her husband-to-be in this very sanctuary. A few years later, her wedding when they walked down this very aisle together after saying their vows. The dedications of their two children.

At the left of the pulpit was a black baby grand piano Barbara had played for many services, special events, weddings, Christmas and Easter cantatas. As she went up to the piano and began to play the opening hymn for the New Year's Day service, her heart filled with anticipation about what God might have in store in the year ahead. The new year was always a special time for her as she thanked God for all He'd done in the previous year and asked Him for a glimpse of what was ahead. Was there a word of guidance or a fresh truth she'd discover today?

When she went back to join Bane and their children in the pew after the singing time, Barbara was eager to hear what her pastor, Reverend John Swails, would preach from the Bible.

As light streamed in through the window of the church, Barbara was about to pray a life-changing prayer.

It began when Reverend Swails picked up his large black Bible and read Luke 5:1–11. As Barbara listened intently to her pastor's reading and to his message, the Holy Spirit stirred within her a surprising sense of what Catherine Marshall wrote about in a book she had recently read entitled *Something More*. Barbara, too, was longing for "something more."

She listened carefully to Luke's Gospel:

So it was, as the multitude pressed about Him to hear the word of God, that He stood by the Lake of Gennesaret, and saw two boats standing by the lake; but the fishermen had gone from them and were washing their nets. Then He got into one of the boats, which was Simon's, and asked him to put out a little from the land. And He sat down and taught the multitudes from the boat.

When He had stopped speaking, He said to Simon, "Launch out into the deep and let down your nets for a catch."

But Simon answered and said to Him, "Master, we have toiled all night and caught nothing; nevertheless at Your word I will let down the net." And when they had done this, they caught a great number of fish, and their net was breaking. So they signaled to their partners in the other boat to come and help them. And they came and filled both the boats, so that they began to sink. When Simon Peter saw it, he fell down at Jesus' knees, saying, "Depart from me, for I am a sinful man, O Lord!"

For he and all who were with him were
astonished at the catch of fish which they had taken;
and so also were James and John, the sons of Zebedee,
who were partners with Simon. And Jesus said to
Simon, "Do not be afraid. From now on you will
catch men." So when they had brought their boats to
land, they forsook all and followed Him. (NKJV)

This biblical scene of the seashore with its fishermen and boats represented all that was familiar to Peter and some of the other disciples. They were working in an ordinary fashion, though there was some merit to fulfilling their daily jobs as fishermen. They were open to hearing the words of Jesus. . .even to sharing their boat for the sake of others.

It was there, in the presence of Jesus on what seemed like an ordinary day, that a miracle happened. Jesus gave Simon Peter a surprising command: "Launch out into the deep. . . ."

This one command compelled Peter past routine logic. It was a command that remarkably thrust Peter into a new revelation of Christ and of himself. We see the evidence of this in the miraculous catch of fish, but also in the spontaneous response of Peter, who fell down at Jesus' feet in repentance: "Depart from me, for I am a sinful man, O Lord!"

That one moment of dynamic confession changed Peter's life forever. It was a dangerous prayer that unlocked his destiny as a follower of Jesus Christ.

Suddenly it was like Barbara was with Jesus and Peter

in the boat. And there was about to be a breakthrough of her destiny.

She was profoundly struck by the picture in Luke and its portrayal of normal, everyday life for Peter and the others: though our lives may exemplify a routine of hard work and wholesome living, Jesus sees far beyond, past those places of familiarity and presumed safety and those tightly held comfort zones.

"Will you launch out into the deep with Me?" she sensed Jesus asking her. She had to respond. Moments after the sermon ended, her arms were draped across the oak-stained altar rail and her knees rested on the green velvet altar cushions. Barbara's dark brown hair fell about her face as she bowed her head, weeping. It was a moment when heaven touched earth and released a remarkable blessing.

As a young wife and mother, she realized the thought of "launching out into the deep" had captured her heart like an arrow that hit its target. She wanted to say yes to God but realized that launching out into the deep required a great deal more surrender of her life. It would require a release from all her inner fears, a laying down of everything secure. It might very well mean going somewhere far away or doing something different than she'd ever planned or considered. It might very well strike a blow to the spirit of timidity that held her back and caused her to cling to the shores of comfortable Christianity. No doubt it would bring change, that much she knew.

She cried out a dangerous prayer to God, seeing how

desperately she needed His help: "Yes, God, I'm willing to launch out into the deep with You! Deliver me from the deep grip of fear that stifles any effort to advance with You. Please give me thrust! Launch me, Lord, out into the deep with You. . .past all my reservations, my timidity, and my comfort zone. Whatever this means, break me free from spiritual mediocrity!"

Luke's recorded story. . .the words of Jesus. . .Peter's response. It was like the deep that calls unto deep, for on that New Year's Sunday morning, those living words called to Barbara. She responded, saying yes to the Lord and releasing everything to Him. In the process, she was changed forever.

The resulting kingdom impact since that day has been varied and exciting. . .and is not over. God opened doors she never dreamed possible—starting with the door of their own home. Thousands of people have come over the years. . .for prayer, Bible studies, personal ministry, and receptions for local Christian college guest speakers. She has offered hospitality to people from around the world.

Though many people have come to Barbara from the nations of the earth, God has also sent her out to many nations to speak, pray, and minister. And she and Bane have had the privilege of founding two ministries.

The first was a denominational prayer ministry in 1982 called WIN (World Intercession Network). Bane and Barbara led the prayer initiative of World Intercession Network for twenty-three years, sending out a monthly WIN Prayergram to over seven thousand people and mobilizing them to pray.

God surprised her when doors opened to serve on the National Prayer Committee and other national and international prayer initiatives.

One of the highlights of her ministry life that called her out of her home church and comfortable surroundings was participating in the intercessory prayer team for a global evangelism conference in Seoul, South Korea, in the 1990s. Throughout this conference, the prayer teams were closeted away in a prayer room for unity among the countries and ministries that attended, for revival around the world, and for an anointing on the messages being delivered in the giant hall where the conference was being held.

The second ministry she never would have dreamed of on the day Jesus called her into the deep was the Joysprings Foundation Barbara and Bane started in 1985. It's an interdenominational ministry whose primary purpose is to provide "Time of Refreshing" retreats as a gift of encouragement for Christian leaders, especially pastors and their spouses, missionary couples, writers, musicians, marketplace entrepreneurs, and military chaplains. It still continues today.

Over the years, countless people have been blessed by Barbara and Bane's loving service to God and people: they've seen emotional healings and physical miracles, as well as relational and financial breakthroughs and provision for churches, widows, and missionaries.

It's amazing what God can do through *one* scripture passage, Luke 5:1–11, and *one* dangerous prayer that *one* timid young woman prayed. It reminds us how important an individual's destiny is to God. He knows what we need and what He's called us to. And He will guide us through His living Word, His Spirit, and our personal experiences—providing encounters along the way that unlock our potential and compel us into new adventures of kingdom life.

All the ways the Lord has ministered through Barbara are wonderful. But what is even more beautiful is the heart and person He shaped in the process, starting with the "something more" she longed for. The deeper relationship with Jesus she has, the presence of the Spirit that people feel when she walks in the room, and the quiet intercessory prayers she prays continually are part of the beauty I and others see.

"Trust yourself and your future to God," Barbara encourages people. "Surrender. With determination, *launch out into the deep with Jesus.* Resist mediocrity and comfort; embrace divine thrust and risk. God's amazing love for you will become evident in the remarkable kingdom journey you will share. . .and many others will also be blessed!"[17]

Chapter Fifteen

HERE I AM! USE ME, GOD!

*No one can sum up all God is able to accomplish
through one solitary life, wholly yielded,
adjusted, and obedient to Him.*
D. L. Moody

A small, dowdy woman in a worn blue coat and hat got off a train in London carrying only an old brown suitcase and purse. Looking up and down the street, she began searching for the office of the China Missionary Society.

When she found the office, she went in and was told to wait. She gazed at the photographs of missionaries serving in foreign fields on the walls, just as she longed to do.

When she was finally ushered into the director's office, she asked, "You *are* going to send me to China, aren't you? I took all the courses at the China Inland Mission School and I studied so hard. I served in the London office of CMS. I'm ready for the mission field and I want to serve in China."

Gladys had already applied to the China Inland Mission Center in her midtwenties and was given a position on probation. However, after her time of service, it didn't lead to a place on the mission field.

This was her last chance.

The director looked at her folder on his desk and then back at the little black-haired woman with a frown.

"You *are* going to use me, aren't you? Surely you are!" she pleaded.

"No, you're just not qualified," he told her. "Our missionaries are very well educated and are specially trained in languages, and you are not either."

"But I can get more training. . . ," she said.

"I'm sorry, we just can't use you," the director said. "You are simply *not qualified*."

For years Gladys had done everything she could to become a missionary. She knew there were millions of people in China who lived in darkness and had never heard the Gospel message. She knew it was God's will for her. She longed to go there and bring the good news of Christ to the Chinese. She'd prepared for the mission field by practicing making speeches over and over in London's Hyde Park. She had ministered to the poorest of the poor in the Bristol slums. She had served faithfully as a Rescue Sister in South Wales. All to be ready for what God had called her to.

She went to the China Inland Mission School, where she labored over the books and studied harder than any other student. But her scores on the examinations weren't high enough to be accepted into that missionary program or any other one.

The only employment she could get was as a nanny and a parlor maid. She'd been born in 1902 into a poor, working-class family and had given her life to Christ as a young woman of eighteen years old. Yet in spite of all her time, effort, and preparation, all she heard was, "You're too old to learn the Chinese language. Your education is inadequate. Your health isn't good enough. You've only worked as a servant. You're a parlor maid."

You are not qualified!

As Gladys walked onto the busy street to the tiny room where she'd stay for the night, her hopes dashed, her head hung down in terrible disappointment at yet another closed door.

"God, here's my Bible! Here's my money! Here's

me! Use me, God!" Gladys cried after the heartbreaking rejection.

Her dangerous prayer echoed Isaiah's prayer in the Bible, in which the prophet said, "I heard the Lord asking, 'Whom should I send as a messenger to this people? Who will go for us?' I said, 'Here I am. Send me'" (Isaiah 6:8 NLT).

Gladys knew that God was asking her to go to the Chinese people as His messenger, and like Isaiah, despite adversities and closed doors, she answered with all her heart, "Here I am. Send me!"

With no other prospects, she went back to the employment agency a few days later, and all she could find was a position as a housemaid for two retired missionaries. Greatly disheartened but determined not to give up, she took the job, performed her duties diligently, and continued saving every shilling she earned to pay for passage to China if she ever got an opportunity to go.

For four years she worked there. Then at age thirty, she heard from her employers of an elderly missionary, Mrs. Jeannie Lawson, in Yangcheng, in the province of Shansi. Mrs. Lawson had ministered in China many years, but she needed a young helper to carry on her work. Gladys wrote to Mrs. Lawson and was accepted. But the elderly missionary could offer no funds to assist her with her travel to China. She would have to get there on her own.

Although she'd saved everything she could, she didn't have enough money to travel by ship as missionaries normally did. So she would have to take a dangerous overland route. The grueling journey would take her across the English Channel by boat and then by train through Holland, Germany, Poland, Russia, and finally to China.

With only her passport and Bible, her tickets, and the very small amount of money she had left after purchasing the train passage, Gladys set off. From the beginning, there was nothing easy about the trip.

The hardships she encountered on the long trip would have made most people turn back. She endured weeks of rugged train travel and two days and nights of walking in deep snow in frigid temperatures, almost freezing to death.

She spent cold, hungry nights on train station platforms all alone in Siberia. There she was interrogated and cruelly treated. Her passport was confiscated. Dreadfully ill, she had to take a detour on a Japanese ship to get to China and then take two long train journeys and several bumpy bus rides before arriving in Tsehchow.

She was not yet at her destination, and Mrs. Lawson couldn't meet her in Tsehchow to guide her the rest of the way. So Gladys traveled on mule trains through wild, rugged territory controlled by warlords to reach the remote mountain village of Yangcheng, where few Europeans had ever been and were rarely welcome. There she met the old missionary, Mrs. Jeannie Lawson, she had come to serve.

Together the two women began planning an evangelistic outreach to mule train drivers in their Inn of Eight Happinesses, as they called it. Gladys helped make much-needed repairs to the inn to restore it to its original use and make places for the muleteers to sleep.

When the muleteers started coming to their "bed-and-breakfast," at night after they had been fed Mrs. Lawson told stories about Jesus and the Bible. They hoped that as they shared the Gospel message with the muleteers, these men would in turn share the good news stories as they traveled hundreds of miles through the villages and towns of China.

Regardless of all the negativity and rejection she'd endured, Gladys was finally *home*. "You just feel where you belong as if you were told," she once said. "For me, it's China."

As China became her home, her daily clothes became the native dress of blue jacket and trousers. She spent hours with the local people in the village, listening to their conversations, and eventually became proficient in the Chinese dialect spoken in that province. She helped Mrs. Lawson run the inn and ministered to many people in mountain villages. As her language skills improved, she learned to tell Bible stories to muleteers as her mentor did.

However, just a year after Gladys's arrival, Mrs. Lawson died. She was left not only with an inn to run and no money, but with overdue taxes that needed to be paid and mission work to do in the villages. In spite of the difficult challenges, she and the cook decided to somehow carry on the work.

This wasn't the first time she had faced huge obstacles. She talked to God about these problems, and the answer came from the highest authority in the territory—the mandarin. He wanted Gladys to be his employee.

She became the official foot inspector of the province of Shansi, with the job of unbinding the feet of every young girl. In this important position, Ai-weh-deh, "the virtuous one," or small woman as the people called Gladys because of her size, could tell Bible stories and share about the love of Jesus and His gift of salvation wherever she went about her job. While unbinding the feet of girls and women throughout the towns, villages, and caves in the mountains, she told them in their own language how much Jesus loved them and how He'd come to save them and bring them into His light.

Gladys had prayed the dangerous prayer, "Use me!" giving all of herself to God. What a testimony to what the Lord can do with one woman of meager education and means when she offers herself to the guidance and power of the Holy Spirit. Through her patient, faithful service, God freed the minds and hearts of countless Chinese people, every conversion a miracle in itself.

Whole villages were converted because of her ministry, and she even single-handedly stopped a violent riot in the Yangcheng prison.

Gladys became fluent in the language, which the mission organizations said she'd never be able to do. As she told the Gospel to people in the villages, she began to discover many cast-off, unwanted children. She adopted several children and brought many under the wing of her care in the inn.

As time passed, Gladys made scores of converts and her influence grew. Even the mandarin became her close friend and ally. He admired her wisdom and strength. She became a Chinese citizen in 1936 and spoke Chinese dialects as fluently as a native. She had defied the odds, survived horrific challenges, and converted whole villages to Christ while years of productive, joyful ministry went by.

And then Japan invaded China and began a mass slaughter of its people. At the same time, China's nationalist and communist armies were engaged in civil war. Her town, Yangcheng, wasn't exempt from the violence. One afternoon the cook, Yang, Gladys, and her growing number of adopted children were praying upstairs in the inn when the Japanese bombed other parts of the town from airplanes. Bruised and injured, she was rescued from the rubble along with the children and got up to aid the wounded in her village.

One day she returned from the mission station in Tsehchow to find the dead bodies of scores of men, women, and children lying in the streets. They had been shot or run through with bayonets by Japanese troops. The streets ran with blood; parents and orphaned children wailed in grief. With the enemy advancing toward them again, Gladys took her own adopted children and all the orphaned little ones of Yangcheng up to the highest village in the mountains to care for and protect them.

After the Japanese troops pursued them into the hills, she had to leave the province with one hundred children orphaned by the massacre and her own children, because not only were the lives of the children threatened, but there was a bounty for her capture, dead or alive. Not deterred, she aimed to get all the children to safety across the mountains in free China. What a daunting journey it would prove to be.

She and the over one hundred children set off on the one-hundred-mile trip on foot through dangerous parts of China. When the children cried in misery from blistered, swollen feet, Gladys led them in singing hymns to keep them going on the trek of miles and miles over the mountains. Exhausted and injured, she became ill on the journey. She and the children had little food and had to scavenge in villages along the way. Sleeping in the open, they were soaked when it rained and thirsty and hungry much of the time.

Nevertheless, as they pressed on, they made it to the Yellow River, a 2,600-mile long river that no one had ever swum across. After a long and sleepless night, she saw no hope of getting the children across the river. It was closed to crossing boats, and she didn't have one.

At that point, Gladys felt like giving up. She was well aware she couldn't walk on water and saw absolutely no way she could take the children any farther.

Listening throughout the night to the distant rifle fire signaling the approach of the enemy troops, she heard the children whimpering in hunger as they lay on the ground. Every crumb of food was good. Despair threatened to overwhelm her as never before in her life.

Feverish, ill, and bone-weary, she looked up at the

dark sky and the stars.

What will become of the children? she thought as she prayed for each one. *Have we come all this way for the Japanese soldiers to come and kill us all? Will we starve?*

The next morning, her daughter Sualan, thirteen, saw how discouraged her mother was and reminded her of the story she'd told them so many times—of Moses and how God parted the Red Sea so the Israelites could cross over it.

"Why doesn't God open the waters of the Yellow River for us to cross?" Sualan asked.

"I am not Moses!" she answered in desperation.

"Of course you aren't. But Jehovah is still God. If He is God, He can open the river for us," she said.

After hearing those words, Gladys saw that the same God who had personally qualified this former poor, unqualified housemaid and transformed her into one of the most beloved missionaries in China could do what was impossible for any man or woman. She still didn't see a way of escape. She didn't know how the Lord would come through, but she knew He had a plan and no longer doubted that He was able.

With her focus shifted from the impossible circumstances to the power of God, she and Sualan knelt at the shores of the Yellow River and prayed that God would open the vast waters for them. Then she got all the children together and led them in singing hymns to keep their minds off their hungry stomachs.

A short time later as they continued to sing praise hymns to God, a Chinese nationalist army officer who was scouting the river heard what sounded like the whirring of an airplane. As he listened more closely, he realized it was the sound of children singing.

After he found them and talked with the small woman leading them, he saw their problem. He called a boat from the other side of the river to get them. After many trips back and forth across the river, Gladys and every child got safely to the other side.

The journey wasn't over. God delivered them across the vast Yellow River, but they faced many harrowing days and nights before reaching the safety of the Christian orphanage in free China. Not one child died.

When she arrived, the small woman collapsed, weakened by malnutrition, typhus, and pneumonia. But not one child died; she'd brought all to a safe and warm place where they would grow up and become an influence for God in China.

Gladys lay deathly ill for weeks following the journey. She never fully recovered from her illness, but once again, God took *all* she'd given Him and infused her with the supernatural courage and strength to persevere in the face of overwhelming obstacles.

She eventually started a church in the region and continued to share the good news with the sick, the imprisoned, the homeless, and the people in villages. Following those years, she traveled back to England to minister for ten years. Her last ministry was in Taiwan, where she founded and ran another orphanage, taking care of the least of these—until her death at age sixty-eight in 1970.

Such is the story of a young Englishwoman, turned down numerous times for her lack of theological or academic training, who just wanted to be useful to Jesus. A woman who was deemed "inadequate"—but not in God's plan! For no matter how big the obstacles or how dire the circumstances, she always had all the sufficiency needed for doing all the things she was called to do—and an abundance left over for every good work (see 2 Corinthians 9:8). And God will do the same for us as we respond to Him and give ourselves to Him fully and extravagantly, as Gladys Aylward did.

Chapter Sixteen

A LIVING SACRIFICE

The adventurous life is not one exempt from fear, but on the contrary one that is lived in full knowledge of fears of all kinds, one in which we go forward in spite of our fears.
PAUL TOURNIER

I sat by Mama's bed in her Baylor Hospital room holding her hand and singing to her one night in the last few weeks of her life. Her once-beautiful dark, wavy hair had fallen out; due to radiation, only a few wispy white hairs remained. Though she was in pain, laboring to breathe with each word, her crystal-blue eyes shone with beauty not even a deadly cancer could take away.

I knew it must be extremely difficult for her to let go of her six children, twenty grandchildren, and everything she loved about life: being at their East Texas ranch, walking up to the lake holding hands with grandkids, and later cooking big meals for them and for other family and friends. Attending Sunday services at their Grand Saline church, caring for her pear trees, and calling each cow by name as she leaned on the fence looking out at their small herd.

As we were talking late that night, I said, "Mama, we will miss you terribly!" and she replied, "I'll miss you and all your sisters and brother so much. I'll miss being there for the birthdays and births and weddings that will come. But soon I'm going to get to see Jesus face-to-face. After praying for you all so many years, now I'll be able to talk to Him about you up close."

She then asked me to write down the verses and songs she wanted to have shared and sung at her memorial service, including "Great Is Thy Faithfulness" and "Special Delivery."

"Now, Cheri, write down that little chorus you've been singing me from Isaiah 61:1–3, because I want it sung at my service." When she'd endured radiation or other treatments and was hurting, she'd ask, "Please sing 'Beauty for Ashes' for me." That wasn't so unusual; my sisters and I stood around her bed and sang to Mama when we visited her in the hospital, just like we had in childhood.

But something about that particular song was special; the words never failed to lift her spirits no matter how much pain she was in.

"Mom, I'm sure the choir can sing those songs, so I'll give your list to the pastor and music minister."

She looked at me as only a mother can and said, "Be sure it's sung at my service, and if no one will, you sing it for me. It's really important. Will you promise?"

Surely I can find someone, I thought and wrote it down.

But when Mama passed from this life into heaven two weeks later and I gave the instructions for her service to the staff, the music minister came by the ranch a few hours later. "Everything's planned just as your mother wanted it. But there's one problem. . .no one in the choir has ever heard of that song."

"It's very easy. It just goes like this: 'He gave me beauty for ashes, the oil of joy for mourning,' " I sang. "Just like the verses in the Bible. I can teach it to you or someone else. Please do this for Mama."

"No one will do it on short notice," he replied. "It's a good thing you know the song, because if it's sung, *you'll* have to do it."

The next morning—the day of Mama's "glorious homecoming" service, as she called it, I woke up heavyhearted and exhausted from all those nights at the hospital. There was a hole in my heart, and I missed her already. She'd been the matriarch of our big family; ever since Papa died when we were young, she was both mother-love and father-love to us all.

Most important, I was neither a professional musician nor in any shape to sing at her funeral. But I didn't want to break my promise.

In those moments of quiet, I said, "Lord, I can't do this! Yet I don't want to let Mama down."

As if a highlighter came down from heaven, I was directed to one particular verse in my reading that morning, Romans 12:1 (NIV): "I urge you, brothers and sisters, in view of God's mercy, to offer your bodies as a living sacrifice, holy and pleasing to God—this is your true and proper worship."

God seemed to be saying clearly, "Just give yourself to Me as a vessel, and I'll do the rest."

Later that day at Mama's service, I stood up, banked by sprays of red roses and white carnations, and sang the little chorus from Isaiah 61:1 that she so loved and wanted friends and family to hear. When I walked up to sing, God gave me His strength at just the moment I needed it. And I wasn't alone; my sweet husband and three children were singing right beside me. I had no idea at the time how God would use that verse and the truth I learned through the experience.

Six years later when my first book came out, we were living in Yarmouth, Maine. The very week it appeared in bookstores, articles I'd written on the subject of children's learning styles were printed in two national magazines.

A few days later, the PTA president called and asked me to speak to the parents of the town's intermediate school about helping kids succeed.

When that first call came inviting me to speak to all the parents, God and I had a little chat.

"Lord! I didn't sign up to speak! I just said I'd write this one book for parents and some articles about kids and learning!" I cried. My stomach was in knots and my heart raced just *thinking* about getting up in front of the parent group to do a presentation.

They'll probably make fun of my Texas accent; people do here all the time, I thought. *I'll get so nervous, I'll forget everything. I can't do this.* "Oh Lord, this is too hard and too scary for me," I reiterated, as if God hadn't heard me the first time. Though I loved one-on-one conversations, speaking to a whole room full of strangers was out of my comfort zone, and terrifying besides.

"*I know. Remember your mother's memorial service?*" God seemed to say when I got quiet. While there wasn't an audible voice, the words were as clear as anything I'd ever heard. "Do what I showed you to do: Romans 12:1—just give yourself to Me as a living sacrifice and I'll do it through you."

I've always been amazed at how much God can say in just a few words.

I did say yes in spite of my hesitation. When I got up to address the Yarmouth Intermediate School parents that first night, my hands were a little shaky and my mouth as dry as it gets on a hot July day when I've been working in the yard.

Yet as I began to talk, I felt an irrepressible sense of joy well up as I talked with the parents about how to help their children achieve in school. And yes, God did it through me as I said yes.

I've been speaking for over thirty years on a variety of topics, and each time I do, I give myself to God quite intentionally beforehand and experience that same joy I felt that first night in Yarmouth, Maine. I also pray that dangerous and wonderful prayer from Romans 12:1 each morning, and when I write books or coach moms in prison to send loving messages to their children. It's become my life verse.

As I sit by the big windows looking at our red cardinals and purple finches fly around the bird feeder in the morning, I sometimes read and pray this verse and the one after it with the words of *The Message*:

> *So here's what I want you to do, God helping you: Take your everyday, ordinary life—your sleeping, eating, going-to-work, and walking-around life— and place it before God as an offering. Embracing what God does for you is the best thing you can do for him. Don't become so well-adjusted to your culture that you fit into it without even thinking. Instead, fix your attention on God. You'll be changed from the inside out. Readily recognize what he wants from you, and quickly respond to it. Unlike the culture around you, always dragging you down*

to its level of immaturity, God brings the best out of you, develops well-formed maturity in you.

ROMANS 12:1-2 MSG

Not that the journey hasn't had twists, turns, obstacles, and difficulties. Once while traveling to a community-wide conference I was keynoting, the little airplane I was on flew into a blizzard smack dab in the mountains of Wyoming. . .and my luggage and makeup never arrived. Or when my husband and I flew across the world for a conference and were supposed to be picked up in Bangkok. Yet we found ourselves at one in the morning alone in an airport where we couldn't speak the language and our driver had forgotten.

I had no idea that dangerous prayer was going to lead me to speak in California and New Jersey; North and South Carolina; Fargo, North Dakota; Washington; Virginia; Hawaii; Nebraska; and almost every state in the nation.

Or that God would really take me up on the first dangerous prayer I ever prayed after a life-changing encounter with Christ in my late twenties, "Lead me wherever You want me to go! I'll go anywhere, anytime, Lord."

I didn't know then God would take me seriously. When He sent my husband, me, and our children to Oklahoma City from Tulsa, I thought, *Really? And I said anywhere!*

But God didn't forget that prayer, and in 1999 I found myself preparing to fly to Chiang Mai in northern

Thailand, a country I'd never even considered traveling to. I was invited to be the speaker at an annual retreat for women from over fifty different mission organizations in the Thailand-Laos-Burma region.

A sense of inadequacy flooded my mind as I started working on what to say for the four sessions of the weekend. *I should be sitting at their feet learning from them,* I thought. *Missionaries are my heroes, and these women have years and years of ministry experience plus extensive knowledge of the Bible. How can I have anything to say to them that they don't already know?* I'd been told some of the women attending the retreat had been on the mission field for more than forty years. That thought almost paralyzed me.

As I sat with my notes laid out before me, the Lord reminded me of the story in John 6 where Jesus taught the multitudes. After hours of His teaching, they were hungry but the disciples said, "Send them away. We don't have enough to feed them!"

But a boy brought his lunch—some bread and fish—and gave it to Jesus. He gave thanks to the Father, broke it, and gave it to the disciples to hand it out to the five thousand gathered there, plus women and children. And there were baskets and baskets left over.

As I pondered that scene of the feeding of the multitude, the Lord said to me, "Take the bread I've given you: the verses of scripture, stories from your life, the lessons I've taught you, and give yourself to Me, and go and share those. And I'll be with you." And He was, all weekend at the women's retreat, every day, with every message, especially when I was scheduled to speak (and did even though I was very ill with an intestinal bacteria that attacked my GI system over the weekend). I shared a message of hope and the power of prayer with sweet Thai mothers on the dirt floor of one of their houses and prayed with them for their children. During that week I also spoke to a large group of Chinese-Thai professionals (with translators of course), to an international school, and to a group of homeschool missionary moms.

I was done. Tomorrow Holmes and I would fly home. Right before bed, however, the phone rang at the Dinkins' home where we stayed. The director of a local orphanage said that the baby with AIDS, little Max, had died in her arms that evening. As he breathed his last breaths in her arms, the Lord spoke to her and said, "Cheri Fuller is to give the message at his funeral service." We'd visited the orphanage the day we flew in and rocked the babies for a while and visited with their dying mothers in an adjoining house on the grounds.

Oh my. I was exhausted by then from speaking eleven times in ten days and was "out of bread," so to speak, but Paula, my host missionary, assured me it was a great ministry opportunity. But it was nothing I ever imagined doing.

As I went to bed that night, I said, "Lord, I've *never* done a funeral before, and I don't have any notes or ideas of what to say. If You don't give me something to share, I won't know what to do or say."

It seems God never runs out of resources. In the

middle of the night, as torrential rain beat down on the roof, He woke me up. I turned on the light and got some paper, and words began to flow into my mind. The next morning when I read it, I realized it was the clearest, most concise message of the Gospel. And I wasn't even an evangelist.

Later that morning we stood around the crib with the orphanage workers, the precious baby boy's body covered in pink roses. After we sang a few hymns, the director nodded at me, signaling to give the message. I read the scriptures and delivered the comfort that the Lord, the God of all comfort, had given me the night before and ended by sharing the hope we have in Christ and the promise of eternal life with Him we have to look forward to after death. An eternal life that this baby had already entered into.

As I spoke, my words were translated into Thai, German, and Dutch. What I didn't know until after-ward was that several German volunteers and eight very secular people from Holland had just arrived at the orphanage to do humanitarian work and were standing with us around the crib. None were believers, and all heard the Gospel message that day.

If I hadn't prayed that dangerous prayer from Romans 12:1 and said yes to God when I felt so inadequate, I would have missed the Thailand journey and also the great adventure in Africa that followed a year later. A young pastor's wife had read my book *When Mothers Pray* and e-mailed me to see if I could pop over the ocean to speak at their women's retreat in September. It just happened I had an invitation in South Africa the following week, so I said yes, I'd be delighted to come.

First Holmes and I traveled to Zambia for the women's retreat on the shores of the Zambezi River in the bush and safari country to share the power of prayer with a wonderful group of mothers. This was their small church's second-ever retreat for women.

When I spoke in the open-air venue by the river, small monkeys they called "local monkeys" started pelting me with nuts—not little peanuts but big, heavy, walnut-sized nuts. When I moved over a little, so did the monkeys. We never found a solution to that problem. But it made for a good laugh for all. I just had to keep speaking while watching out for the next flying nut.

The lodge was on the riverbank as well, so when we looked out, we could see hippopotamuses floating in the water. Those hippos looked cute but were dangerous. So were the ones in the zoo, but they were inside giant fences. We were told that more humans were killed by the hippos than the crocodiles. Duly noted.

"And don't go outside on your porch in the dark!" the ladies warned us. That night and every night when we were safe inside our wood and native-grass-thatched-roof chalet, we could hear the hippos on our porch, chomping on the shrubs for their bedtime snack. So glad we'd been warned.

A few days later we flew to South Africa to speak at a women's conference. Getting to meet my Afrikaans and British sisters-in-Christ, along with women from the Zulu, Tsonga, and Swazi tribes was a highlight of our time there.

I had no idea that giving myself as fully as I knew how would take me to Brazil a year later to keynote a nationwide conference on igniting the next generation of children for Christ. And to Singapore to share with Islamic, Christian, and Buddhist parents how to motivate their children to learn. I didn't know when I started the first book I wrote and those that followed that they would reach people in other countries who would invite me to come—because moms and dads around the world wanted encouragement for how to help their children be successful and get good educations, how to pray for them so they could grow up strong in faith and have an opportunity to live out their potential.

I love and believe the truth of Ephesians 2:10 (NLT), "For we are God's masterpiece. He has created us anew in Christ Jesus, *so we can do the good things he planned for us long ago*" (emphasis added).

So He had planned all those speaking trips beforehand, the close ones and the across-the-ocean ones, and even the little event for parents at that first public school. In fact, God has shaped and wired each one of us from the inside, prepared us through life circumstances, and equipped us with education and His guidance to do the very things He wants us to pursue—even if they are way out of our comfort zone.

I love that as we pray dangerous prayers and put feet to those prayers, we begin to discover that following Christ and His plan for us is truly the greatest adventure in the world and more fun than you can imagine or dream of.

Chapter Seventeen

A COSTLY PRAYER

If we really want to love, we must learn to forgive.
MOTHER TERESA

On Christmas morning Cynthia, her husband, Buddy, and their two sons sat in their pajamas under their brightly decorated tree that shone with twinkle lights. As they sipped cups of hot cocoa and ate cinnamon rolls she'd gotten up at 6:00 a.m. to bake, she thought about the surprise she had for her father-in-law and hoped he'd like it.

Several piles of presents wrapped in red, green, and gold paper with carefully tied bows were spread around the tree. When they gave the signal that their boys could start opening, they dived into their presents with an excitement that always amazed her, especially since they were teenagers now.

Jack, her father-in-law, sat in a recliner near the tree in his khaki pants and red-and-blue-plaid shirt, drinking strong black coffee. He opened his gifts: two pairs of bulky brown socks, the kind he liked, a new flannel shirt, and a western novel to read in the long winter evening hours when he was alone in his house.

Then after he'd finished opening presents, he saw a wrapped box with his name and a big red satin bow over the wrapping paper. His hands, rough from years of building things, untied the ribbon and looked inside the box. He was visibly moved.

Inside was a Christmas letter from Cynthia, his daughter-in-law, explaining that his gift was a letter every week that she would write him during the whole year ahead. His blue eyes twinkled, and his lined face radiated a joy she hadn't seen in a long time as he read her letter. Since his wife had died, Jack, now in his mideighties, lived out on the Illinois River by himself. It was three hours away from his son and family, and he *loved* getting letters.

After opening his gift, he gave Cynthia a big hug.

As long as she'd known him, Buddy's father had been an alcoholic who was full of bitterness. In fact, she'd never seen him sober. He didn't start drinking heavily until Buddy was a senior in high school. Before that, he'd been a great dad, involved in his son's life, always attending his football games. A real family man.

There was still a side to Jack that was playful. He liked to make people laugh and could rattle off endless jokes. He also loved playing games and cards. But there was another side that was absolutely bitter from past hurts as a child. He'd been abandoned by his father in his early years.

But he'd done well in business and was a good provider. As a brilliant geologist, he'd worked for a long time for a leading oil company.

Things went well for many years, but at a certain point, the head of the corporation wanted to drill in Cuba. As he and the board of directors made a business plan to move ahead, Jack was resistant and never went along with it. In fact, he was belligerent about what a big risk it was.

The boss pressed ahead, built rigs in Cuba, and began drilling. When Castro took over, however, the oil company went broke, just as Jack had feared and warned them about. The boss committed suicide, and Jack was demoted.

He never forgot that injustice and responded to the unfair treatment with a deepening unforgiveness. So over the years, the hurts, abandonments, betrayals, and injustices had stuffed his emotional bag so full of anger and bitterness that most of what came out of him was pure venom.

If something ticked him off or he didn't get his way, he blew up in a fit of rage. He didn't have any relationship with or interest in God. So in his later years, he spent every evening from 5:00 p.m. on drinking beer and wine. Every day he wrote an angry letter to the government about the wrong things he thought they were doing.

After Cynthia and Buddy's marriage, she prayed for her father-in-law often. Through the years, she tried in various ways to witness to him. Occasionally she wrote letters to Jack, sharing about Christ's love. She did her best to be loving and thoughtful toward him when they were together. But after a while, Jack became more and more antagonistic about Christ and told her *never, ever* to mention Jesus again, whether in a letter or in person.

That's when Cynthia began praying, "Help me show Jack Your love."

For a couple of years, the Lord impressed on her before Christmas to give him the present of a letter a week for a year. But she wrestled with that idea because she didn't want to write fifty-two letters if she couldn't say anything about Jesus, about what they were doing at church, or about the ministry she and Buddy were involved in.

Finally she decided to be obedient to God. She wrote out the Christmas letter and said she was going to write him one letter a week for a whole year.

Pleased by Jack's response when he opened her box and read her letter, they continued with Christmas dinner and visiting with other family members who dropped in that evening and had a wonderful time together.

Then on the weekend after Christmas, company arrived—a whole family of six people. Cynthia cooked for the whole bunch and served three meals a day, in addition to keeping an eye on the kids and entertaining their guests. So she didn't write the letter to her father-in-law until Saturday of the first week of January when the company left.

Her letter was full of news of her boys, the basketball season they were in the middle of, how they'd been doing in high school, and what was new with Buddy and his business. It was a sweet letter that told him she loved him and she hoped he was doing well, and she closed with "Take care of yourself."

Several days later she was sitting at her kitchen table with the mail in front of her. She opened a letter addressed to her from Jack and saw her crumpled Christmas letter stuffed into the envelope along with his.

Then tears filled her eyes as she began to read lines and lines of nasty, angry sentences full of profanity and accusations that she'd already broken her promise and that she was a terrible, selfish person.

Cynthia wrote him again and sent the Christmas letter back in the envelope. In it, she said she understood his feelings and that she'd written the first week as she'd planned, but because of their guests staying for five days, she'd written at the end of the week. Surely it had gotten to him by now. She apologized sincerely for the letter arriving late, told him she was truly sorry, and asked him to forgive her.

In her mind, Cynthia had thought he would accept her apology and give her another chance, that these loving letters would melt his bitter heart. But nothing even close to that happened. It was as if her letters opened a can of venom she never could have foreseen.

She wrote Jack every week, but every letter he sent to her said mean, hateful things: that she was the worst mother he'd ever known, that her children were spoiled brats who behaved terribly. "When your boys get to college, you'll still be wiping their bottoms," he railed.

She knew there was some truth to what he said. She did spoil her sons, but they were good boys who were well behaved and kind most of the time and who loved their grandfather. They'd won citizenship and good character awards at school and were leaders on the sports teams they played on.

Every week it was the same, only the letters got worse. As the months wore on, his personal attacks hit her like a big red wasp that stings over and over. It wasn't only that he was critical; the meanness of his words was overwhelming. She didn't know someone could be filled with such hatred.

"I saw this fat woman on a TV show and she reminds me of you," he said in one letter and then elaborated on how overweight and ugly she was. It took a few days to get over the hurt and anger she felt from the vile attack and curse words he used. Every letter felt like a slap on the face.

In May of that year, he started in on Buddy and wrote about what a horrible, worthless son he was. That was the last straw for Cynthia. She knew that her husband was one of the kindest and most unselfish people she'd ever known. And that despite his dad's alcoholic rages and the awful way he treated his family, he was a deeply loving son.

That day after reading Jack's profanity- and hatred-filled letter, she said to the Lord, "That's it. I'm not writing him another letter."

The Lord asked her, "What was your prayer? What did you ask Me?"

The words of her dangerous prayer came right back to her mind. "I prayed, Lord, how can I show Jack Your love?"

"That's exactly what I'm doing," God answered her. "I'm allowing you to show him My love, a love that when it's being reviled, does not revile back. That blesses those who persecute you. That turns the other cheek. A love that loves the unlovely and doesn't return evil for evil but instead returns good. A love that forgives and keeps loving no matter what."

In that moment she realized that she'd thought she'd show her father-in-law God's love by doing something sweet: writing loving letters every week. She thought he'd respond in a positive way and his heart would be touched by the kindness of her letters.

Instead it opened him up to tear her and her children and husband apart.

But Jesus had something else in mind—the shaping of Cynthia's heart to be more like His, a heart that unconditionally loves and forgives others, even His enemies who maligned, mistreated, and crucified Him when He did nothing to deserve it.

She realized that she'd have to forgive Jack every week and needed the Lord's help for that. After one of his cruel letters arrived, it would take her a couple of days to let Jesus heal her pierced heart and forgive the terrible things he said about his own grandchildren and son. . .and the hatred he spewed on her.

So she continued writing loving, newsy letters every week for the rest of the year. As the months passed, she began to see Jack through God's eyes instead of her own, and He gave her more of His unconditional love for him. She realized that he was a very wounded man who'd never received the love of Jesus into his life.

She wrote the letters until the very last week of that year, but never received a positive word back from him. She had thought surely if you love someone and you're kind, then they can't help but respond—eventually.

That didn't prove true in this situation.

Jack never changed. He never softened. They spent every holiday with him and saw him every couple of months. But they never knew how he'd behave, how angrily he'd react if anyone made him mad. A few summers later he broke his hip and their son Barrett and his friend traveled to his home to help him for a week. But he chewed the boys out and told them they were losers even while they were caring for him.

This was fifteen years before her father-in-law died. A couple of family members were by his bedside with him during his last hours. They were all so hopeful that he would accept and receive God's love; he'd surely had plenty of chances, but no one knew if he did.

Yet through the months of writing and forgiving, Cynthia learned a huge lesson: that Christ's love can't be defined by people who love you back—but by those who reject you. In Matthew 5:11–12 (NIV) Jesus said, "Blessed are you when people insult you, persecute you and falsely say all kinds of evil against you because of me. Rejoice and be glad, because great is your reward in heaven. . ." When they reject and revile you, you have an opportunity to show the Lord's love by continuing to love them back. And by forgiving them over and over even when they keep hurting you.

"Lord, how can I show Jack Your love?" A costly and dangerous prayer indeed.

Chapter Eighteen

SAYING YES TO GOD

Yes, it is God who works in you.
And yes, there is work for you to do.
Yes, the Spirit empowers you to do the work.
And yes, you do the work.
Francis Chan

One day Louise Montgomery was waiting for her car to be repaired in a small town in Maine when into the auto shop strolled Alison Kelley, and the two women who had never met began chatting. Soon they discovered that although they were twenty years apart in age, they had much in common, especially the fact that both were strong believers in the power of prayer. The two became prayer partners.

Alison, a registered nurse, often spoke to Louise about her volunteer work at a shelter for the homeless in Boston. She described the people who had nowhere to go at night, who hadn't had a good warm meal in weeks, whose clothes were not sufficient to keep them warm in the bitter cold weather—and the relief she saw on their faces when they got to enter the homeless shelter. When they got to take a shower, have a bowl of hearty, hot soup and bread, and hear a message of hope—the gratitude they expressed overwhelmed her.

As they talked and prayed over the weeks and months that followed, Louise became convinced God wanted her to open a shelter for the homeless in Portland, Maine.

When God called, Louise said yes even though she and her husband, Claude, were in their midseventies, an unlikely age to embark on such a mission. In addition, they knew little about reconstruction of an old house or helping the homeless.

Claude was an acclaimed marine and landscape artist who grew up in Maine. Louise was raised in New Jersey and summered in Maine. There she met her future husband when they were playing croquet on

Peak's Island at the age of three. They didn't marry until their late twenties. Then as a young couple they traveled widely while Claude was studying art in Europe.

Together they raised a son and two daughters, and as Claude had studios in both Maine and Tulsa, Oklahoma, they lived both places at different seasons of the family's life. In Tulsa, Claude painted portraits of wealthy oil magnates after World War II and during the oil boom.

He also painted portraits of L. L. Bean and political and business leaders. He had completed commissioned portraits of governors, secretaries of state, philanthropists, and federal judges. Right before President John Kennedy was assassinated, Claude had been at the White House for the president's sittings and was in the middle of painting his portrait.

Louise and Claude loved spending time at their home on Indian Point in Georgetown that overlooked the ocean. Georgetown was located on an island near the mouth of the Kennebec River and offered plenty of privacy and the scenery to inspire Claude, as well as a studio with the ideal light for painting. Both loved to sail, and Louise graciously hosted friends and family who visited them.

Yet they were willing to leave this idyllic place to serve the homeless in the inner city? Yes, because God called.

Louise and Claude had a life savings of approximately $50,000. She hoped to find a big house they could make into a unique shelter for homeless people and call it the "Friendship House." Louise thought surely they could find the building and fix it up for $50,000 to be a place where their guests (she never intended to call them clients, only "guests") could find refuge and the help they needed to get sober and on their feet again.

Portland had a pressing need for another shelter and certainly more homeless people than the existing shelter or the city could deal with. Yet when Louise and Claude talked to their friends and others in the community about the idea of finding a house to restore and open as a shelter for the homeless in the inner city, they heard nothing but negative feedback:

"You don't know what you're getting into; it'll never happen."

"You're too old to do something this huge," others said.

"You'll never find a house for that money," their real estate agent told them.

Despite the naysayers, God had given Louise a dream and a mission, and she began combing Portland for a house with the energy, determination, and joy with which she did everything. For a while it wasn't looking promising. Houses were far too expensive to even consider on the booming Maine market, even old run-down and shabby ones.

Yet find a house they did: a fourteen-room, dilapidated Queen Anne structure that most people wouldn't have touched. With broken-out windows, boarded-up doors, the house had been vandalized numerous times. Once a lovely neighborhood, it was now a relic of faded glory.

And while the house had been beautiful long before, it

was now terribly broken like the people Louise wanted to help.

Restoring it was a huge, seemingly impossible project, but as she prayed, Louise felt directed to ask for help from the Cumberland County Jail. At first her requests were refused. She may have been a bit discouraged, but Louise didn't give up.

After many objections, the county officials finally agreed to lend the jail's manpower. That was an adventure all its own! With the inmates' help over a period of months, this elderly couple restored all the ceilings and floors, replaced large broken windows, replastered and painted every wall, and painted the whole exterior of the three-story house. Many obstacles presented themselves, but after prayer they always found a way. And God provided.

Claude traded one of his paintings for appliances. Their daughter gave a new furnace. For weeks, Louise went to churches of all faiths, speaking about their mission and inviting them to join her. She returned with contributions of blankets, furniture, food, and money. Yet more funds were needed in order to open the shelter. She wrote to all the alumni at the university she had graduated from and asked for donations, which came pouring in.

The night before Christmas Eve 1985, Friendship House opened its doors to serve the homeless with a graciousness and love their guests never dreamed of—and Louise and Claude lived right there with them.

A few of the first guests were former inmates of the

jail who'd helped them do the reconstruction. Some were like Jenny, a woman in her fifties who'd been living in a boxcar under a bridge. One night during a blizzard she arrived at Friendship House and ended up staying for the winter. Other people stayed two weeks to two months. Most were helped to find a job and get in recovery from addictions, and also were encouraged to save money for a new start.

A young woman came to Louise after roaming cross-country, trying to resolve her drug problems. The local rehab center had no space, and with the dirty clothes she was wearing, she wasn't welcome anywhere. But Friendship House opened its doors to her. Former guests often returned, even after they were out and making it on their own. Like the couple who helped Louise begin a free day camp for inner-city children one summer.

These past residents knew they were always welcome to come back. Some sent donations. Sometimes they wanted to help out. But more than that, they came back because they felt like they were part of the family.

Louise told me her husband had suffered from alcoholism until 1969, so they both felt a special compassion for many of the homeless who were recovering alcoholics and addicts.

Their mission: to express the love of God through Christ to the poor and disadvantaged by providing a safe home where hope and healing are extended to those who are broken spiritually, emotionally, or physically.

Today, Friendship House is still helping men

overcome their addictions. My husband and I and our children were there to help give a party for the guests and serve dinner with our friend Louise. On other occasions we brought food or mittens and gloves for her guests. I loved riding with her as she drove through Portland or along the Maine back roads up to their place at Indian Point, meeting with people who could help the guests at Friendship House. I was always inspired by Louise as we talked about the amazing power of prayer and the many ideas she had for better serving people at the shelter on Brackett Street.

Most of their guests had never had a real home before, and many called Louise and Claude Mom and Pop. She told me, "I asked Claude why the Lord waited until I was in my seventies. He answered that I wouldn't have been ready before." Although they lived an interesting life, Louise considered the founding of Friendship House the most rewarding work she'd ever done, and she was always grateful to God for His miracle-working power, guidance, and help.

One important thing I learned from my elderly friend is that although the project or mission God calls us to may be different from hers, the same God has a plan to use each of us for His great purposes—no matter our age or stage of life. And He promises to reveal that plan if we're looking, listening, and willing to put aside our agenda and follow the Lord's.

He also has pledged: "I will instruct you and teach you in the way you should go; I will counsel you with my loving eye on you" (Psalm 32:8 NIV). God will provide the guidance and show you the steps to take just as He did for Louise, but He wants you to do your part to say yes and then step out in faith, doing the work He calls you to do. Claude died in 1990, and Louise continued her tireless work on behalf of the homeless until she died two years later. The ministry she and Claude founded in Friendship House has lived on long after they entered heaven—and it is still blessing countless broken people with hope, healing, and renewed lives.

Is saying yes to God a dangerous prayer? Think of all the people in the Bible whose yes made a difference, though they faced peril and adversity: like Noah, who said yes to the Lord when He asked him to build the ark. Or Moses, who said yes to God when he knelt at the burning bush without knowing the danger and challenges that lay ahead in delivering the Israelites out of Egypt and leading them through the wilderness.

Mary, the mother of Jesus, said a resounding yes to God. So did the disciples who left everything behind to follow Christ. When we say yes, we partner with the Lord of the universe in His mission on the earth, whether that is in a small work or a grand ministry. What could be better?

Chapter Nineteen

WHEN *YOU* ARE THE
ANSWER TO YOUR PRAYER

*Sometimes all it takes is just
one prayer to change everything.*
UNKNOWN

Gary leaned on his desk after school and groaned, his heart aching as he prayed for the steady stream of teenagers that had flowed through the gym where he had been teaching all day. For ten years he was a high school coach and teacher in a rough inner-city school, working with kids who were really at the bottom of the heap. It was the 1970s, and urban decay and poverty were all around them. Not only were local structures deteriorating, but families were deteriorating as well. The majority of the students had not had the same two parents during their short lives.

Many of the kids came to school high on drugs; some were involved in gangs. Some of their parents had just taken off and left the children. Other teens had incarcerated or drug-addicted parents, and when the parents were absent, the kids had to work to put food on the table for their younger siblings and be the mother or father of their families—all while trying to get a high school education.

Some of the students lived in rat-infested houses with a parent or relative who wasn't able or willing to support them emotionally, spiritually, or academically. So they struggled.

Gary taught physical education, but he and his wife, Joy, could see the students needed much more than just athletic or physical skills. They needed Jesus and a community of people who loved them.

Gary and Joy started praying for a church to bring the kids to where they would be received as the precious, unique creations they were. Their prayer was, "Oh God, please show us the church where we could bring our young friends, a place that would see the real treasures they are and nurture them and show them Your heart and Your love."

They looked in the community, searching to find a church like that. For three years they continued petitioning God to show them a community of believers who would love and welcome these challenging, lost teens. Yet with all their searching and praying, they never found it.

As time went on, Gary accepted a full-time staff position at the church they attended in a neighboring community, serving as the leader of home groups and Sunday school. He invented a title for himself, "program director," because he definitely didn't want anyone to call him a pastor!

After a few years, he said, "I'm going back to teaching." However, when he checked with God about that plan, the Lord said, "You'll rot if you go back to teaching."

Gary was only thirty-five years old, and he thought that was too young to rot.

Although he and his wife had never been the slightest bit interested in planting a church, they were led from much prayer and guidance to do exactly that. They were both trained as teachers and never imagined they were going to be pastors. They didn't consider themselves bright shining stars. They had no experience in church-planting or running a church ministry.

As they were beginning, so many times they came to a point where they said, "We don't know how to do this,

God," and each time He brought them just the right people who had the wisdom they needed.

As the church grew, someone in the community said, "Oh, that church; they'll take *anyone* there!" The speaker meant it as an insult, but they took it as a compliment. For Joy and Gary realized the church they'd planted was just the kind of church they'd been longing for and praying for all those years before but never found: A community of believers who would embrace the long-haired teenagers who came from poverty, who didn't have the right clothes, who were tattooed, pierced, or rough-looking. A community of believers who would love the kids struggling with addictions and broken-ness. A place where they weren't just tolerated but welcomed, where people would think it was a real joy that these young people had come to Jesus and joined the family of God.

Finally, a place they'd prayed and dreamed of where they could bring their friends who wouldn't be welcomed anywhere else. Now these teens could be loved and esteemed as diamonds in the rough, with spiritual parents and grandparents who believed in them, who wanted to be there for them and nurture their faith.

God brought this unique church to birth through ordinary people—Joy and Gary.

What a blessing to be the answer to their own prayer. And what a privilege to be the hands and feet of Jesus to countless lost and hurting youth who found new life. People of all ages in that community were drawn to the light emanating from that small church plant that became the first Vineyard church in Canada.

Joy and Gary have continued to serve together in ministry, and God has used them around the world. For twenty-seven years they pastored, and for seventeen of those years they led Vineyard Churches Canada. They are now officially retired but still love to inspire people to believe that the Lord can use ordinary people and work through them just as Jesus did in the New Testament stories.

Chapter Twenty

A LIGHT IN THE DARKNESS

The only Christ for whom there is a shred of evidence
is a miraculous figure making stupendous claims.
C. S. LEWIS

The digital clock on Emily's bedside table flashed 4:00 a.m. She pulled herself upright, her nightgown damp with perspiration. *Another nightmare.* The darkness outside the window seemed to have crept into her soul. She heard nothing from the normally busy street below.

New York City, the city that never slept, didn't bother to wake up with her in these nighttime vigils. She flipped on the light and slipped into her robe as she headed to her studio. She sank down onto a stool with a sigh and ran her hands over the smooth wood and cold metal of the sculpture she'd worked on until midnight the night before.

Too soon, she glanced at the clock and saw that it was time to get ready for her 6:00 a.m. workout at the gym. After donning exercise clothes and tying her tennis shoes, she headed downtown. She shook her head as she thought about Lauren, the woman she'd met in the locker room. Lauren called herself a Christian. What a strange word to Emily, who was an avowed atheist.

Christian. In all her thirty-seven years, Emily had never met one until now. She shuddered as she thought of the stereotypes she'd seen on the news.

Christians, she thought, *are part of a dangerous political party. Those ridiculous religious freaks who think they know everything. I can't stand them. Lauren doesn't seem dangerous. But she is really different.*

That morning after their workout, Emily said, "Lauren, you seem like a pretty cool person. You must be mistaken about being a Christian. You're not anything like those bigoted political types on Fox."

"But I *am* a Christian!" Lauren explained. "And it's not political. It means I love God—I love my Savior, Jesus Christ."

Emily cringed, tempted to put her hand over Lauren's mouth so nobody would hear those words. They were in a downtown New York City gym full of healthy, liberal-minded, smart people like herself. Few of them would welcome some wacko who called herself a Christian.

So again, with sincere concern, Emily tried to set her friend straight, "Shhhh. . .you don't know who you're lining yourself up with. And don't say that word, *Jesus*!"

In spite of what Emily saw as Lauren's strange religious beliefs, the two gym buddies turned out to be good friends. They saw each other at 6:00 a.m. five days a week in the women's locker room.

Bit by bit Emily poured out her soul to Lauren because she listened with extreme kindness as if she really cared. Emily tried to expand their relationship to include other activities she and her friends took part in: political causes, downtown rallies, defending abortion clinics, or the many parties she gave.

But Lauren always said no, and Emily began to understand how different they were. They talked about a lot of issues that touched them both deeply. They clearly disagreed about many things, but Lauren never became cruelly angry with Emily the way most people who disagreed with her were.

Emily fought battles in the world, in both her personal and her professional lives. She continued her art career, working every day in her studio. She tried to fill the emptiness inside with alcohol, lovers, art, and relationships. But nothing filled the hole.

Because Lauren had great insight about life and people, however, Emily continued to talk with her about her hurts and fears, her friends and lovers. She told her about her causes and beliefs, her paintings and the art world. Emily watched Lauren go through struggles, too, but she always seemed to trust in that God of hers when she had problems.

One morning in the locker room, Lauren gave Emily a Bible. She was mortified. It was big and red and wouldn't fit inside her gym bag. They'd been friends for over a year by then, so she felt she couldn't refuse the Bible even though it was an unwanted gift. Didn't Lauren know she didn't believe in any God at all?

Emily saw something else in Lauren that day, like how much she loved the book she presented to her with such love and joy. In giving her that Bible, it was as if she was giving her a part of herself.

Of all the things Lauren told Emily, the one she remembered the most was that in no uncertain terms God loved her. Hearing that made her cry.

Wiping tears out of the corners of her eyes, she said, "Lauren, I'm sure you believe that God of yours loves you, and I'm sure He could love you, but if He exists, He could *never* love me."

Over the next four years their locker room discussions continued. In 1993 Emily married one of her lovers and should have been on top of the world, but she wasn't.

In fact, she was just the opposite. She had a deep, dark secret no one knew: she was filled with tremendous, overwhelming fear and despair.

While awake and asleep Emily also wrestled with unanswerable questions. *Who are humans? Why are we here, spinning around on this little planet, killing each other, accumulating things, and waiting to die?*

She couldn't stop thinking about a riddle: "What would you do if you were trapped in a room with a hungry lion and there was no way out?" "Pray, I guess," was the commonly shrugged-out answer.

Pray, Emily thought. *What kind of answer is that? That's no answer!* Yet she felt trapped inside that room, and the hungry lion was life itself. It was clear that no matter what she pretended, she was always only one accidental bite away from utter fallibility or destruction. And in the meantime people she loved were dying. . .of AIDS, of old age, and she was growing older. . .all for what?

For years Emily believed an existentialist theory that goes something like this: All humans, in order to stay functional, must live in a constant state of denial. If we really perceived, at any one moment, our reality, which is that we don't know who we are, why we are here, when we are going to die, or what happens to us after we die, we would all go running stark-raving mad in the street because we couldn't handle that awful reality for one moment.

But she *did* perceive that awful reality. And she couldn't handle it and was finally tired of trying. The rest of her deep, dark secret was that she wanted off this planet, and bad.

Friends and family would have been shocked by the suicide note she had written:

> *I'm very sorry that I have misled you, but I am profoundly unhappy. I know I said that beauty is worth living for. I know I implied that the mysteries of life are great fuel for art. But the truth is, I'm not strong enough to handle this despair any longer. I am afraid all the time. I am losing my ability to hide my true self. I am very ugly inside, and I do not want any of you to see the horror that I know.*

When Emily confided the contents of her suicide note to Lauren, she expected panic. Instead all she got was a calm, steady gaze full of love. "Emily, would you consider coming with me to my church next Sunday?"

She was dumbstruck. *How in the world is going to church a solution?* She squirmed and shifted her weight, started to speak, but nothing came out.

"Church?" was all she could say.

"You might like it. You just might find some of those answers you've always looked for."

"I don't have to pray, do I? Or go up to the front or do anything weird?" she asked. She thought prayer was dangerous. She had seen people on TV praying in flowery religious language. It made her sick. Besides, praying to a God she didn't believe in could destroy all the atheistic philosophies she'd lived by for years.

But Emily realized she had nowhere to turn. She was at the end of her rope.

"Okay," was all she managed to say. They arranged to meet the following Sunday morning.

Throughout the church service, Emily felt self-conscious and out of place. Besides being uncomfortable with all the hymn singing, she couldn't understand what they were talking about. She couldn't connect with the prayers that were said. It was like hearing a foreign language. None of the words made sense.

However, during the announcements (when for a few moments it sounded like they were speaking regular English), one of the pastors described a series of classes called "Discovering Christianity," which started the following Sunday. The description caught her attention. When she got home, she told her husband about the course.

"Are you crazy? I don't want to go to any church service," Neil said. After thinking about it for a while, he added, "But I'll check out the classes with you if you'd like."

The following week the three friends attended "Discovering Christianity." The teacher explained answers to questions Emily had never thought of asking and ones she'd wondered about for years. She and people in the class asked him questions, and she was amazed to hear him substantiate everything he said with objective facts.

What she was hearing was remarkable, and quite

possibly more important than anything she'd ever been taught before. . .that Jesus was a real, historical figure who really had walked this earth and called Himself God, thereby making Him either a liar, a lunatic, or who He said He was.

But how could that be? Emily kept thinking. *If He really called Himself God, if by chance He was and this was real, why wouldn't the whole world know about this? Why would I never have heard about it before?*

Throughout the following week she thought about everything she'd heard. *Could it be? Could Jesus have been God? Surely that would be impossible! If that were true, then that would mean there* is *a God, and that would change everything! Is it really possible?* She wrestled over and over with those thoughts. She couldn't get them off her mind.

The night after the second class, Emily had a dream she never forgot.

In the dream she was talking on the phone with her mother and telling her she'd like to come home. To her shock, her mother interrupted her and said, "No, you cannot come home."

Emily tensed up. "*What do you mean* I cannot come home? I want to come home! I need to come home! I have to come home!"

"No, you cannot," her mother answered. "In fact, the truth is, if you do come home, your home will not be here. I will not be here. There is *no home.*"

"What?" Emily screamed. "Don't say that!" In the dream she threw down the phone and ran outside in terror, desperate to find her home. She ran into what seemed like an endless gray mist. As she blindly raced, not knowing which way to go, she became hideously ugly and repulsive. Her skin began to fall off. She became a monster, a terrible monster. Her worst fear was death, and she was becoming death personified.

In this horrible state of fear and desperation, lost in the world and lost from herself, a figure stepped out of the mist and wrapped his arms fully around her. At once she was filled with three feelings she had never known before: total peace; complete safety; and deep, incomprehensible love.

Emily gasped and sat up in bed, heart pounding and wide awake.

It was Jesus.

She looked over at her sleeping husband, undisturbed by her epiphany. *What do I do?* Then she remembered something the teacher had said the day before about asking Jesus into your heart.

So she said out loud but soft enough not to wake her husband: "Jesus, I know You're real. Please come into my heart and please lock the door from the inside and *please don't ever, ever leave.*" Then she slid down under the covers and fell into the most peaceful sleep she'd ever known.

The next morning when she woke up, Jesus was the first thing on her mind and the words "He's real!" burst out of her lips. She couldn't wait to get dressed. Her husband eyed her curiously because she was full of joy, a feeling he had *never* seen in his wife. It was also a feeling she had never experienced. She wanted to run out into the streets and look at everything as if for the first time. She wanted to sing and shout, dance and leap for joy. Yes, as an atheist, she'd prayed a dangerous prayer—but now she was filled with gratitude that she had.

There is eternity. Jesus is real! He is exactly who He said He was. God exists!

She grabbed the big red Bible Lauren had given her four years earlier. Now she opened it up and couldn't put it down. Instead of spending all her morning hours that day working on her watercolors and paintings for the gallery showing, she spent them in the presence of Jesus. She drank in the words of the Bible as a thirsty person who had found a cool stream.

When Emily told Lauren what had happened to her and how she'd given her life to Jesus, Lauren squealed with delight and immediately said, "Oh, wouldn't it be great if your husband could know Jesus, too?"

"Lauren, Neil isn't like me. He's really into martial arts and Buddhism, and he's not plagued by fears like I have been. In fact, he's the least afraid person I've ever met."

Six weeks later they had taken all six classes and the first of another course on foundations of the Christian faith. One Sunday after class, Neil said he wanted to stay for church.

That same night as they were getting into bed, he said, "Emily, I've seen how much you have changed, and it looks so good. I wasn't sure what to do, but I heard myself saying, 'Lord, I'm crazy for her. I love her so much. Lord, I think maybe You've called on her and I want to be where she is. Would You come and get me, too?' "

She threw her arms around him and tears flowed down both of their faces. As an artist, Emily knew she could create many things and that she had a gifted imagination. But could she have imagined Jesus? No way.

Up until the moment Christ appeared in her dream, she had been repelled by His very name. After having been given a glimpse of His absolute perfection, she knew it would have been impossible for her to invent what she didn't know. She knew everything of life was tainted with some flaw, some limitation.

Until she met Jesus.

Jesus came alongside her. He put His arms around her and revealed Himself to her. Total peace, complete safety, and incomprehensible, perfect love belong to Him.

No longer was Emily enslaved by her art career. No longer was her identity dependent on whether critics wrote positive reviews of her art exhibits. She now felt so thoroughly known by Christ, who knew her as an artist and a woman, so affirmed by Him in her inner being, she didn't feel driven to prove herself. She was known and loved by Him, and that was what really mattered.

Before she met Jesus, the first thing she did each morning was to grab a cup of coffee, go into her studio, and slave away at her work. Now she went into the Master Artist's study, eagerly picking up God's Word and reading it for hours. It didn't make her less productive. Instead, she sensed new inspiration and creativity welling up from within and flowing onto the canvas.

She also began to reach out to others in the art world and show the love of Christ to them as Lauren had done for her. And that same Bible that had seemed like nonsense and gobbledygook became Life to her. Jesus was her refuge, and she knew now she was safely hidden in the Rock, no longer living in terror or despair.

Emily knows what fear is. It is to be trapped in a room with a hungry lion. It is to be trapped within life, instead of living it. It is to be trapped in overwhelming darkness with no way out. She wouldn't go back there for anything. She knows what freedom is and where it comes from. She read in the Bible that perfect love drives out fear. Since she first met Jesus, she has gone through innumerable trials and losses, but through them, she has found that knowing Jesus is immeasurably greater than anything one could possibly think or imagine. She knows He brought her out of the darkness into light and freedom, and whoever He sets free is free indeed.

Chapter Twenty-One

STEPPING OUT

*The initial call to discipleship was a call to adventure.
The early disciples were called to leave their families and
the comfort and security of familiar ways and places,
to go they knew not where, and to do they knew not what.
Day by day they discovered that life was a great adventure,
and that every hardship and every setback was a
doorway to new service and maturity.*
KEITH MILLER AND BRUCE LARSON

I hope you've been inspired by the stories and adventures of the people in this book. Perhaps reading them has prompted some thinking or made you reconsider a nudge or a quiet whisper of God's Spirit.

Do you want to impact the world for Christ, or your community with God's love? Do you want to live out the purpose you were created for? Then let me encourage you that the dangerous prayers you may be prompted to pray may well open a door to a whole new future—especially if you're ready to follow when God says "Go." If you launch out on the adventure this prayer leads you to, I guarantee you won't be plugging along on autopilot or bored with life.

Rather than experiencing boredom, you'll live the greatest adventure of a lifetime. You'll need to depend on the Lord even more when you're on the edge of adventure. I promise you that God has something for you that is greater and much more fulfilling than comfort and ease, and it may be a destiny and purpose you never thought of.

Even one line of the Lord's Prayer, "God, may Your kingdom come," can be a dangerous prayer. While it has been prayed in churches and cathedrals all around the world millions of times, it is often prayed in a somewhat rote way. Yet "God, may Your kingdom come" is dangerous if you really mean it, because you're surrendering to God's plans and letting go of your own.

When we pray this kingdom prayer, we are giving over the center of our life to the King of kings, who truly is meant to be at the center. And rather than clinging to our way or following our own will, we embrace God's plan for our lives. The outcome could mean sacrifice. The journey may bring uncomfortable situations or perhaps some adversity.

But it's so worth the ride!

The rewards are out of this world: First, getting to experience a joy in life that this world cannot give, a by-product of being used by God. Second, discovering what you were made for, what your purpose is, and why you were designed the way you are. Third, gaining the opportunity to depend on and trust God with all your heart, perhaps more than you ever have. And last, making a difference in the people and the world around you.

Where do you start? Consider the following questions that may help you process what you've read in this book and move you in the direction the Lord wants for you.

- What's pulling at your heart that you see and care about even if no one around you seems to?
- What is something that, when it comes to your attention, sticks tight and won't leave your thinking—yet other people don't notice it?
- What breaks your heart?
- Which story in *Dangerous Prayer* impacted you the most or spoke to you?

Now let's look at the way you're created and how that can lead to the calling on your life:

- What do people keep saying about you that affirms who you are and how God wove you together?
- What experiences have you had in life that give you a heart or burden for an issue or group of people?
- As you consider your answers to the questions above, what if anything do you feel fearful about?
- What dangerous prayer or call from God might you resist out of that fear or caution?

Now let's put God in that equation:

- What do you think about God?
- What flaws in your earthly father or other spiritual authority have obscured your view of God?
- How faithful has the Lord proved Himself to be in your experience and in your reading of the Bible?
- If you are already on the journey that resulted from a dangerous prayer, how has God guided you so far? What help or light has He put on your path to direct you?

Do know that I am not encouraging anyone to pray selfish or unwise prayers cloaked as dangerous prayers, such as, "Lord, I feel like I need to divorce my wife so I can be free to serve you or go to another country." If the dangerous prayer doesn't line up with God's principles and Word, avoid praying it.

Be assured that God will find ways to affirm your call. And He will confirm or nudge over and over until you're ready. Be patient with the Lord *and* with yourself, because there is a right time for everything, and we don't always know that timing—how comforting to know that God does!

For example, in my story "How Prayer Led Me to Prison," I shared with you that I prayed, "Lord, send me to prison to help the mothers pray for their children." That was in about 1995, yet the door to actually do that didn't open until 2008, thirteen years later. Since by then I was not a spring chicken, I found the timing puzzling. When I asked my longtime friend Melanie about why God waited so long to call me to this mission, she said, "It took that long to get you ready!" Several other stories in this book show the principle of waiting for God's timing as well. Which ones are they?

If you worry, "Am I making this up?" when you hear the Lord calling you to step out and pray a dangerous prayer, don't be disturbed. If the idea truly is from His Spirit, it won't go away and He'll keep reminding you or bringing situations or people across your path to direct you. Share the idea with a trusted friend or counselor, but rather than banking on others' opinions, keep tuning in to what God is saying. Which story illustrates this principle?

In the meantime, don't force things to happen. If you've committed your prayer to God, He's not going to let you miss out. If it's not supposed to happen *right now*, rest in the fact that there will be a best time He has in mind.

Be aware also that how *you think* things are going to look when the answer to your dangerous prayer happens may not resemble how it actually turns out when it's fully formed. Go back and reread Katherine's story, "The Box of Chocolates" (chapter 10). It may be just the seed of an idea you have, but the Lord will shape that call and He is faithful.

All God needs is for you to be willing and to keep saying yes to Him. And for you to take time to *listen* to God's Spirit and keep reading His book, the Bible. Since Jesus is the living Word, He often chooses to speak to His people through His Word. So when you sit down to read the Bible, pray as little Samuel did, "Speak, Lord, for Your servant listens."

The colors will get filled in and God will move things forward in His time as you continue to be obedient. "I want to do Your will more than I want to do mine" is a powerful, dangerous, and wonderful prayer that the Lord honors. And it's beautiful to see His will and purpose for you unfold in the process.

It's always helped me in all the adventures and adversity of life to remember that there is no panic in heaven, and that no matter what happens, God is still on His throne. And He doesn't have problems, only plans.

Consider reading through this book with a friend or your spouse, and then discuss the following questions and your responses.

What dangerous prayer do you sense the Holy Spirit inviting you to pray? Write it here.

What "yes" are you ready to say today to God? Write it out here.

God has "created each of us in His image to do something that no one else on earth was called here to do," says Danny Cahill.[18] As we pray dangerous prayers that focus more on God's purpose than our own, our lives will be changed forever.

God bless you as you step out, pray dangerous prayers, and do what you're called and designed to do.

If you have a dangerous prayer story, e-mail me at cheri@cherifuller.com. Share your story (no more than 1,000 to 1,500 words, please). Please include your contact information. If we do another *Dangerous Prayer* book or blog, I may write and ask for permission to use your story. Thanks!

—*Cheri Fuller*

ENDNOTES

1. Billy Hallowell. "Hollywood Actress Says This is 'Most Dangerous Prayer You Can Pray'" www.TheBlaze.com/?s=roma+downey+dangerous+prayer

2. Herbert Lockyer, *All the Prayers of the Bible* (Grand Rapids: Zondervan, 1959), 29.

3. "Women in Prison: Why Oklahoma leads the nation," by Oklahoma Watch, May 12, 2011, http://oklahmawatch.org/project.php?pid=1, 1.

4. Ibid, 1.

5. The Messages Project was founded by Carolyn LeCroy, www.themessagesproject.org. For more information, see www.oklahomamessagesproject.org.

6. Leigh Ann Bryant, *In My Defense: An Unlikely Romance, a Deadly Gunshot, and a Young Widow's Road to Redemption* (Franklin, TN: Authentic, 2013); www.leighannbryant.com.

7. Hannah Hurnard, *Hinds' Feet on High Places* (Carol Stream, IL: Tyndale House Publishers, Living Books, 1975), 127.

8. Adapted from Hannah Hurnard, *Hinds' Feet on High Places*, 305–311.

9. Ibid., 93.

10. Quotes in conversation between Jesus and the woman at the well are adapted from *The Message* paraphrase of the Bible.

11. Herbert Lockyer, *All the Prayers of the Bible* (Grand Rapids: Zondervan, 1959), 223.

12. Oswald Chambers, *My Utmost for His Highest* (Westwood, NJ: Barbour and Company, 1935) 244.

13. hollywoodprayernetwork.org.

14. Oswald Chambers, *My Utmost for His Highest* (Westwood, NJ: Barbour and Company, 1935), 52.

15. Herbert Lockyer, *All the Prayers of the Bible* (Grand Rapids: Zondervan, 1959), 60.

16. Ibid, 62.

17. My deep appreciation and thanks to Barbara James for allowing me to adapt the story she wrote for this book.

18. Danny Cahill, quoted on nationaldayofprayer.org/ can-you-relate/April, 2015. Danny is a speaker and author of *Lose Big*, and winner of TV's "The Biggest Loser."

ABOUT THE AUTHOR

Cheri Fuller is an internationally published author of over 45 books. A gifted speaker, she has presented throughout the US and other countries, bringing messages of hope and encouragement to live life to the fullest, find joy in an often difficult, upside down world, build loving connections with family and friends while impacting the world around them with prayer and action. Her articles on family, prayer, relationships, and children have appeared in *Family Circle, Guideposts, ParentLife, Better Homes and Gardens, Faith and Spirit,* as well as numerous other publications, and she has appeared on many radio and TV programs.

Cheri is a former Oklahoma Mother of the Year and serves as the Executive Director of Oklahoma Messages Project, a nonprofit that provides life-giving programs for children of incarcerated parents.

She and her husband, Holmes, have three grown children and six grandchildren. To contact her or learn more about her books and speaking, visit www.cherifuller.com, and their mission to kids of incarcerated parents, www.oklahomamessagesproject.org.